The Most Beautiful

Thames & Hudson

HUGH PALMER

Villages of Spain

WITH 274 ILLUSTRATIONS IN COLOR

Acknowledgments

Spain's extraordinary culture takes a long time to understand, but a short time to enjoy. During my attempts to get to grips with this huge country, I was often daunted, but never down-hearted: the delightful welcome of its people always made me feel at home. I had invaluable help from the staff of the Spanish Tourist Office in London, in particular Claire Turner and Pituca Caton, and from their counterparts all over the different regions and provinces of Spain. My progress was speeded by the fluent interpretations of my talented wife Hoonie, and the invaluable suggestions of Piers Plumptre. His sister is my god-daughter Hermione, to whom this book is dedicated, with love.

© 2003 Thames & Hudson Ltd, London
Text & photographs © 2003 Hugh Palmer

First published in hardcover in the United States of America in 2003 by Thames & Hudson Inc., 500 Fifth Avenue, New York, New York 10110

thamesandhudsonusa.com

Library of Congress Catalog Card Number 2002116940
ISBN 0-500-51128-4

Printed and bound in Singapore by C. S. Graphics

Contents

Half-title page
Siesta time in the village of Candelario (Salamanca), framed by a characteristic grey stone window surround.

Title pages
Montilla stands at the the heart of the wine-producing region of Montilla-Moriles, south of the city of Córdoba.

These pages
The villages of Spain from light to shade (left to right)*: the vaulted entrance to the medieval church of San Esteban in Sos del Rey Católico (Zaragoza); the Arco de las Monjas of Vejer de la Frontera (Cádiz), one of the white villages of Andalucía; the Puerta de la Villa, the fortified gateway opening into the village of Pedraza (Segovia); a forbidding corner of the castle at Ribadavia (Ourense), in the valley of the Minho.*

Introduction 6

EASTERN SPAIN

THE HEART OF SPAIN

ANDALUCÍA

NORTHERN SPAIN

Useful Information

INTRODUCTION

STAND ABOVE ALBARRACÍN, underneath the huge mass of its defensive walls, and look down. A tableau of Spain's amazing history lies before you, in the dramatic view of the ancient village as it hangs on to a sheer cliff above the curving river Guadalaviar. A Roman fort stood here, and a Celtic settlement before that. The walls, straggling across the windswept hills of this remote corner of southern Aragón, have stood here since they were built by the Moors in the tenth century. The Beni Razin dynasty chose this to be the capital of their *taifa* kingdom, a stronghold against raids by warriors of the rival Almohad clans. Less than a hundred years later, as the Reconquista spread across Spain, they were forced to cede control to a family of Christian nobles from Navarra, the Azagras, leaving just their name behind them. The Azagras were able to hold out until 1300 as an independent state, refusing the constant demands for fealty made by the kings of Aragón. Once under their control, Albarracín, gaining wealth from the manufacture of cloth, became a bishopric, with the construction of a great cathedral in the sixteenth century, and a magnificent episcopal palace two hundred years later.

Such grandeur can seem in contrast to the diminutive scale of the village itself, crammed in tightly inside its defensive walls. You enter through one of its original gates, still more suited to carts than cars, before strolling down the cobbled lanes towards the Plaza Mayor, between the ancient houses. Their wooden balconies almost touch above your head, the resulting gloom adding to the wonderfully medieval atmosphere. It is not merely because so much of the fabric of this age-old place has survived: it is also because the sensitivity with which it has been restored and presented has avoided those false touches that can break the spell of timelessness. Not that such respect for the past has compromised the present-day comforts on offer. Find your way to the Calle San Juan, and step into the Casona del Ajimez. Here, an eighteenth-century mansion has been

Albarracín (Teruel) (opposite) is a microcosm of Spanish history: once a Roman fort, then a Moorish stronghold, later an independent Christian enclave, and finally a bishopric – with a magnificent cathedral and episcopal palace. The surviving defensive walls date from the Moorish occupation.

The riches of rural Spain are varied indeed. The main church, Santa María la Coronada (above), of the Andalucían village of Medina Sidonia is crowned by a magnificent seventeenth-century tower. In southern Castilla, near Piedrahíta (Ávila), sunlit meadows – even in November – provide a startling contrast to a sudden surge of barren mountain (opposite).

exquisitely restored by a local man whose pride in his own efforts needed an audience to share his passion, so he opened his house as a small hotel. Inside, the style is restoration purist meets twenty-first-century hi-tech. In both the respectful looking back to history and traditions, and in the imaginative looking forward to the future, his efforts are a symbol of the new wave of tourism in Spain.

The country is of course not a new destination for visitors from abroad. Those determined enough have always found a way to cross that classic geographic barrier, the Pyrenees: from the faithful in their thousands who have made their laborious way to the shrine of Santiago de Compostela, to the modern pilgrims who soar blithely over the mountains in their millions, on the way to the south. But they have often found an ersatz Spain on offer along on the shores of the Mediterranean, a tawdry product, more a factor of cheap land and quick profits, where popular English-language culture has been brought in to make visitors feel 'at home'. This in a country whose own culture has so much to delight and teach us! True, the classic cities were always there, huge bastions of history and culture, but, in general, Spain was considered a wasteland, where the grimness and poverty of the less accessible places put off all but the most adventurous visitor.

It was left to intrepid writers to spread the word, such as Gerald Brenan in Andalucía, and Norman Lewis on the Costa Brava, who settled in their chosen villages and stayed long enough to appreciate their fascinating and complex character. Nowadays, the new generation of developers is no longer concentrating its efforts on increasing the ribbon of high-rise coastal resorts; instead, the hinterland is being opened up as new highways plunge through mountains, leap across valleys and career across the vast hallucinatory plains of Castilla, in an orgy of spending funded, for the time being at least, by the European Community.

And what a wild diversity of terrain Spain can offer! From the balmy estuary of the Guadalquivir, where at Sanlúcar de Barrameda, the worthies of Seville sought relief from the annual inferno of summer in their home city; up into the lofty, mountain villages

*S*igns of past grandeur abound in even the smallest Spanish village. Pedraza (Segovia), with a population of less than five hundred, has several magnificent houses embellished with the crests of the great families who lived there in the seventeenth century.

bring you high into the Sierra Nevada, where the last of the Moors clung to their isolated communities; up the east coast to discover El Palmar, sitting precariously on its freshwater lagoon, whose paddy fields have for centuries produced the rice for the region's famous *paella*; on to the Costa Brava – the 'wild coast' – whose fantastic Dalí-inspiring rock-scapes shelter the neat fishing village of Cadaqués; into Navarra, where quiet villages, with huge-eaved houses looking as if transplanted from the Alps, are tucked neatly into the lush valleys that run down between the foothills of the western Pyrenees; across to windswept Galicia, whose merchant houses with their giant glassed-in balconies still gaze westwards to the wild Atlantic coast; lastly, to confront that huge inescapable fact of Spain's geography, the Meseta, the vast central plateau which dominates the country. The climate of this great plain, described by meteorologists as 'continental', can be extremely harsh: freezing in the winter and broiling in summer. The terrain is unforgettable, of endless horizons and a barrenness which give it a surreal beauty. Despite the labour of centuries, it has remained ungenerous in cultivation. Villages such as Pedraza and Calatañazor sit on their rocky outcrops, gazing out over its emptiness. The proud feudal and military might of these outposts, in contrast to the strange emptiness of their former dominions, is unforgettably moving.

Some of the villages included in this book, slumbering in their remote corners of the countryside, have remained mere specks on the population map; others have grown to sizeable proportions, and come to be surrounded by quite untraditional housing or even industrial estates. But rarely has the essential character of the centre changed, despite the agglomeration that may have grown up around it. The way the Plaza Mayor is laid out, with trees and walks overlooked by fine old merchants' houses, is the way the inhabitants like it to be, and that is the way it hopefully will always stay, to delight travellers to come.

It is not only isolation that has preserved these ancient places. There are strong traditions, a respect for a past that has often been brutally tough, ensuring the preservation of these wonderful treasures in their pristine state. Also, the very idiosyncracy of Spain's history has kept the heritage alive. Only the most Euro-centric world-view would see Spain as having stagnated in her apparent isolation on the other side of the Pyrenees, cut off from the ebb and flow of events in the rest of Europe. Compared with the Pyrenees, the Straits of Gibraltar were easy to cross, and from the eighth century the Muslim invaders poured across in waves, and very nearly succeeded in colonizing the whole peninsula. It is difficult to think of any other invading force that mingled its own culture in such a consensual way with that of the conquered. Together with a considerable population of Jewish settlers which had spread all over Spain in the Middle Ages (who, together with the last *moriscos*, were not expelled until the end of the fifteenth century) they created a culture – in literature, learning, poetry, music and, above all, architecture – that is an indissoluble part of Spain.

The rechristianizing Reyes Católicos, Ferdinand of Aragón and Isabel of Castilla, intent on bringing the whole of Spain under their centralizing power, were also a great cultural force, but certainly not in the same spirit of laissez-faire. Their campaign of ethnic cleansing and religious persecution was brutally efficient, with the confiscation of goods and land helping to provide the means to finance global expansion. Spain ended up with an empire, the *conquistadores* treating the indigenous people of their new colonies in the Americas with the same mercilessness that their monarchs displayed in the home country. Galleons packed with booty sailed back to Spain, and the monarchs and prelates alike embellished with silver and gold the palaces and cathedrals, the massive emblems of absolute power. It was not to last.

Under the Habsburgs, the fortunes of the Spanish armies changed, its proud armadas ran aground, and the empire slipped away. It is hard for a nation to lose the status of imperial power, and Spain lost her way for centuries.

The last century saw the nadir of long-drawn-out decline, as the country inflicted on itself the most bitter of defeats in the Civil War

Though subject to varying fortunes, the Church is ever-present in rural Spain; symbolically, the ornate towers of the huge monastic complex of Guadalupe (Cáceres) rise above the roofs of the village houses (above).

The climatological extremes of northern Spain inspire scenes of preparation for harsh winters: storing timber in Bárcena Mayor (Cantabria) (top) and grain storage in quaintly decorative structures in the farming communities of Asturias. A more benign weather pattern nurtures the white wines of Galicia, a wonderful accompaniment to the delicious seafood of the region. These vineyards cluster around the fine Baroque church of Santa María de Beade near Ribeiro (A Coruña).

of 1936. All attempts to rule Spain from the centre have brought pain to its people, all have eventually failed, and hopefully that of the unlamented fascist regime will be the country's last. Many hopes are pinned to the success of the emergent democratic state that has gone from strength to strength in the triumphant end of the last century. A bold federal system has so far managed to satisfy many of the regional aspirations of the now autonomous regions, and the economy is booming.

Yet this confident re-entry into the modern world has not brought about the loss of important traditions. Try the following simple experiment : utter the words, 'Se habla ingles?' in the most friendly way possible. Back will come, in the huge majority of cases, the frustrating but entirely affable monosyllable: '¡No!'. Even for the best-educated Spaniard, there is more than enough going on in his or her culture, without the need for a deluge of imports.

Spain demands to be experienced on its own terms: if, as a visitor, you make the effort to meet its people halfway, their legendary hospitality will be redoubled in your favour. Happily for anyone who enjoys good food and drink, the pleasures of the table are a particular passion for the Spanish, and you will be in very good company if you choose to explore the wonderful and varied cuisine of the country. Spain is now abuzz: a fresh and enthusiastic flowering of its culture is adding to the legacy of its long and extraordinary history. In the villages, where so much of the past is preserved in bricks and stone, and where local people are now reinterpreting their traditions and deciding their future, fascinating adventures and discoveries await the traveller.

EASTERN SPAIN

A suitably surreal combination of boat and tree (above) marks the approach to the house of Salvador Dalí at Port Lligat (Girona). One of the great vistas of northern Aragón provides a backdrop to this oddly isolated cross on the edge of fortified Sos del Rey Católico (opposite).

SPAIN'S MEDITERRANEAN COAST, most immediately associated with high-rise hotels lining long, and very crowded, stretches of beach, does not immediately reveal itself as a fertile hunting ground for the seeker after the traditional Spanish village. But there are ample rewards for perseverance: Cadaqués in the far north of the rugged Costa Brava, has, with the help of its artistic coterie, retained the character of the simple fishing village that Salvador Dalí and others discovered in the 1930s. Peñíscola, isolated halfway down the Costa Blanca, crowns a high promontory, thus remaining aloof from the mushrooming development along the littoral. South of Valencia, El Palmar sits in its own lagoon of paddy fields, utilizing the ancient marshlands of the Albufera to grow the rice that made neighbouring Valencia famous as the birthplace of Spain's national dish – *paella.*

Inland, the explorer of the plains and rugged sierras of Aragón and Cataluñya can discover wonderful medieval villages, in which inspired restoration programmes have succeeded in developing the tourism potential of each community by enhancing rather than suppressing its individual culture. The Spanish have a taste and a flair for these matters, and the delightful presentation of such recently restored treasures as the episcopal palace in the remote village of Albarracín easily makes up for the disappointment sometimes felt when the less inspired efforts of an earlier generation have resulted in a dowdy assemblage of objects in a regional museum.

*I*n the wooded hills of the remoter
parts of Cataluña hidden
villages like tiny Rupit (Barcelona)
can count on unbroken pastoral calm.

Albarracín

TERUEL

This sixteenth-century house by the Portal del Molina (above), its roughcast exterior relieved by elaborate wrought-iron grilles and sculpted coat of arms, was one of the first to be built outside the walls of Albarracín, which still overshadow the town (opposite).

THE RIVER GUADALAVIAR is not much more than a stream as it meanders past Albarracín, but it has still managed to carve a deep gorge out of the local sandstone. The spectacular cliff on which the village sits makes the modest river look curiously out of scale, an effect emphasized by the imposing grandeur of the buildings which hang in a cluster from their high perch. Fortunately, the road from Teruel has its own tunnel through the rock beneath, so that there is little to disturb the magical atmosphere of the medieval streets. These twist and clamber between the overhanging upper storeys of the ancient houses, which lean crazily towards each other. Many of these houses were built from the local sandstone, called *rodeno*, from its reddish colour. The plaster walls of the village are washed with a red gesso produced nearby from the same material, so that the whole ensemble harmonizes perfectly with its rocky surroundings.

Always a strategic military centre, Albarracín became an important Muslim stronghold after the region was overrun by the invaders from the south.

They built the extensive fortifications along the ridge above the village to reinforce the defensive capabilities of its eagle's-nest position, alone no guarantee of impregnability from attack from neighbouring hills. These *murallas*, all in an excellent state of preservation, provide a good excuse for a clamber up the hillside to enjoy a grand view of the village's spectacular setting.

Albarracín's pre-eminence in the district reached a high point in the eleventh century, when the ruling Beni Razin dynasty (from which the name Albarracín comes), made it the capital of their independent kingdom, during the last years of Muslim rule. The village retained its status after it was handed back to the Christians: in addition to its existing parish churches, a giant cathedral was built and, beside its cloister, an episcopal palace was added in the eighteenth century. This has recently been carefully restored, so that the generously proportioned windows now permit the present-day visitor the same wonderful views down the gorge which must have refreshed the spirits of many a pampered cleric in the past.

*A*lbarracín is a village of both intimate charm and magnificence. Simple small houses of timber-frame construction combined with characteristic rose-coloured roughcast, and embellished with decorated balconies, lie under the shadow of the towering cathedral. The latter's huge vaulted nave, dating from the sixteenth century, terminates in a majestic organ (above). Outside, the scale of the place seems suddenly to shrink: the Casa de la Julieneta (opposite) lies pinched at the angle of two medieval lanes, one leading up to the church of Santiago and the other down towards the Plaza Mayor.

*I*ts protected position on the sierra
(opposite) made Albarracín a
natural choice for fortification for
successive waves of invaders: Celts,
Romans, Moors and Christians. In
the tenth century, the Moors further
strengthened the position of the
settlement by raising defensive walls,
the muralla, along the ridge above
the village (below). These were
later put to other uses – here, as the
support for a lean-to house (right).

Alquézar

HUESCA

THE APPROACH to the village of Alquézar could hardly be more dramatic. The road climbs up the blind side of a neighbouring hill, and suddenly reveals the towering mass of the twelfth-century castle dwarfing the cluster of houses, huddled below. Upon this same limestone crag the Moors built their original *alcázar*, but nothing of this remains. It was demolished by the king of Aragón, Sancho Ramírez, after he completed his Reconquista at the end of the eleventh century.

Despite the small size of the place, which is home to fewer than three hundred, it is easy to lose one's sense of direction. The network of tiny streets runs hither and thither, often disappearing under covered archways connecting the upper storeys. It was said to be possible, in times past, to cross the village without once descending to ground level. From the close confines of this little warren, it is exhilarating to climb up through the outer portal of the castle's defences and follow the steep pathway which zigzags up the slope of the citadel, which is bounded on two sides by the deep canyon cut by the Río Vero. The views from the castle battlements over the surrounding limestone massif are spectacular, those downwards, vertiginous.

To consolidate his control of the area, Sancho Ramírez established a religious community here, La Canónica de Santa María, whose duties were defensive as well as religious. Of their church inside the castle walls, just the southern cloister survives, with its charming Romanesque arcading. Scenes from the Old Testament are carved above the capitals, and more recent wall paintings from the New Testament decorate the walls. The rest of the church of Santa María is a Baroque replacement dating from the sixteenth century, spacious and not overly ornamented. It makes a perfect ensemble with the older cloister, which forms its atrium.

The houses of the village are dominated by the sixteenth-century Colegiata (opposite), *built over the remains of a Moorish citadel, the* alcázar, *from which the place takes its name. Many of the houses were built so close together that tradition had it that it was possible to cross from one side of the village to the other without descending to street level. Unusually, the Calle Baja* (above) *is relatively open, although the houses lining it still seem to grow into each other.*

The north side of the Colegiata's cloister (opposite), *alongside the church, is very evidently its oldest part; the splendid capitals are decorated with scenes from both Old and New Testaments* (right). *Viewed from outside, the cloister appears loftily perched on the towering mass of the south façade of the Colegiata* (below), *where it abuts a square tower originally built for defence but now housing the church bells.*

Overleaf
There is more embellishment of the cloister in the form of frescoes, dating from the fifteenth and sixteenth centuries (p. 28), *including this Baptism of Christ. At the west end of the church, there is an unusual effect of space and light* (p. 29); *note the model houses in the side-chapel.*

Besalú GIRONA

The village's famous dog-leg bridge (below) dates from the beginning of the eleventh century; the fortified towers were added two hundred years later, one to form the Portal del Pont, the main point of access to the village. Within Besalú tradition is still strong: the Tuesday market on the Plaça Llibertat (opposite) is centuries-old.

BESALÚ'S idiosyncratic bridge, which hops from stepping-stone to stepping-stone across the river Fluvià (necessitating a sharp left turn a third of the way over), has been the principal way into the village since its construction in the eleventh century. In the village's most prosperous era, when it was under the control of local grandees, it was rebuilt to incorporate a fortified gatehouse, at which travellers and their goods were required to pay their *pagus*, or toll, before they were allowed to enter. Despite the benign appearance of the shallow river, the bridge has been washed away and rebuilt a number of times; it suffered what was hopefully its last major catastrophe during the Civil War, when part of it was blown up. Since then it has been restored to its pristine splendour, and it is a lovely way to enter one of Spain's most unspoilt medieval villages. It leads not into one of the larger plazas, but into its most intimate and intricate quarter, the *Call*, or Jewish ghetto. Ancient records show that the Jewish community here had sufficient influence to be given a special royal dispensation to build a synagogue, but no

trace of it has been found. What has been unearthed as recently as 1964, and restored, is a great rarity: a bathhouse for the Jewish ritual of purification, dating from the eleventh century.

Life goes on in a gently mercantile way in the streets and squares of Besalú – it feels little changed, especially on Tuesday mornings, when the two main squares fill with market stalls. The Plaça Llibertat is the smaller of the two, and the more ancient, with deeply vaulted arcades running along two of its sides. The larger Prat de Sant Pere is a more spacious affair, being really the recycling of what was the burial ground of the huge monastery of Sant Pere. Only the monastery church survives, but it is quite a survival – a huge stately edifice rated among the most important twelfth-century buildings in Spain. If its elegant façade appears to lack a sufficiently important portico, seek out the little Hospital de Sant Julia round the corner. Its Romanesque doorway, hugely out of proportion to the modest building, is thought to be a further example of recycling, lifted from the monastery after its dissolution.

*M*arket day presents an ideal opportunity to catch up on local news around the Plaça Llibertat (this page). *Less animated, the street named after an eleventh-century lord, the Calle Tallaferro (opposite), leads through the old Jewish quarter to the site of the former castle.*

*T*he highest point of Besalú was once the site of its castle, stronghold of the
counts of Girona. Nothing of the past building now remains except
for the Colegiata de Santa María, built from the stones of the ruined castle at
the end of the twelfth century. However, when secular power ruled, the counts
used to levy toll on travellers at the outermost tower of the bridge (opposite).

Cadaqués GIRONA

THERE IS A HEROIC AIR about any *finis terrae*, the ultimate point of a country which protrudes into the ocean. On the eastern side of Spain, this distinction belongs to the Cabo de Creus, which forms the very last outcrop of the Pyrenees. Although the sea that washes around it is the relatively benign Mediterranean, as opposed to the thundering Atlantic, this cape is as ruggedly rocky as its Brittany cousin. Appropriately, the little village that has been crammed on to the rocky spit is all to do with fishing. The miniature Corniche which curls crazily around the coves and tiny beaches is lined with excellent seafood restaurants in which the visitor can sit in the sun, enjoy the fruits of the sea and watch the craft from which they were caught bobbing about in the safety of the little harbour. Behind, the oldest streets form a warren of stairs and cobbled alleys, plastered to the side of a tiny, ancient citadel, topped by the shapely Renaissance church of Santa María.

This unpretentious fishing village, surrounded by bizarre rock formations and bathed in a mysterious reflected light, exercised a strange attraction for the artists who first started to arrive there in the second half of the nineteenth century. Later, Salvador Dalí fell for the remote charms of Port Lligat, a cluster of fishermen's cottages and a tiny beach clinging to the extremity of the Cabo de Creus.

Dalí's plans for the place seem to have been more than acceptable to the local community, bemused by the ingenuity with which their fellow Catalan promoted himself. The artist's house is now immaculately preserved as a museum, complete with the huge mirror that he had mounted at an angle to the wall of the antechamber to his bedroom to indulge his fantasy of being the first man in Spain to see the rising sun.

The village sits on a steep hill, crowned by the church of Santa María, from which a network of streets and stairways lead down to harbour level (above and opposite). A terrace along the south front of the church allows a view along the Riba d'en Pitxot.

*L*ooking out towards the calm Mediterranean, the old quarters of Cadaqués fold round the harbour, dominated by Santa María.

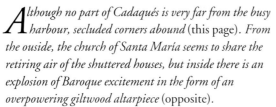

Although no part of Cadaqués is very far from the busy harbour, secluded corners abound (this page). *From the ouside, the church of Santa María seems to share the retiring air of the shuttered houses, but inside there is an explosion of Baroque excitement in the form of an overpowering giltwood altarpiece* (opposite).

A devoted, if selective, disciple of Freud, Salvador Dalí proclaimed his 'paranoia-critical' aesthetic to be the key to the meaning of his paintings. An understanding of his principles no doubt helps to appreciate the decoration of his own home at Port Lligat (these pages).

Overleaf

T he tortured rock formations of the coast around Cadaqués are themselves suggestive of a master surrealist at work (p. 44). They are, however, punctuated by tiny sandy inlets, as at Platya S'aranella (p. 45), where the local fishermen can beach their modest craft.

L'Arenel

Deià MALLORCA

THE DRIVE TO DEIÀ is delightful, as the road follows the ins and outs of the pretty west coast of Mallorca, but if the idea is to go to this hilltop haven to relax, there is an even better way to get there. An old-fashioned train, dating from the 1920s, runs up to nearby Sóller from the relative bustle of Palma, the island's capital. As though aware that gentle decompression is good for the system, it takes its time to clatter up through groves of orange and lemon trees, whose branches brush the windows of the old wooden carriages, releasing warm scents and splashing the interior with shade and sunshine. Sybaritic delights of a more modern order await the well-heeled at a luxury hotel, the result of the amalgamation of two farmhouses opposite the village; but any visitor who catches fine weather will find refreshment in the simple beauties of the place.

All the houses are built from the local stone, and the resulting colour scheme of blues, greens and ochres, as the eye travels over the terraced olive groves to the sea, is breathtaking. The Moorish settlers here first laid out the system of open irrigation channels, which have been in use ever since. As well as the olives, almond and fruit trees have been planted in every little scrap of fertile soil that could be persuaded to cling to the side of the rocky hillside with patient terracing.

Deià itself sits on a steep hill, clustered around the old church, close to which the most famous of its relaxed foreign habitués, the poet Robert Graves, is buried. The view inland takes in the peaks of the lofty Sierra de Tramuntana, whose highest point, the 'Teix', rises to over a thousand metres just behind the village. To complete the rest cure, there is good bathing at the village's pebbly cove.

*T*he dramatic beauty of Deià's setting in a fold of the hills
 – terraced to accommodate the olive groves –
proved irresistible to generations of artists and writers who
took up residence there (opposite). Every corner, usually seen
against the backdrop of the Sierra de Tramuntana, holds
delights: houses and walls in local materials, seemingly
springing from the landscape (left *and* above); a tiled panel
in the local church (above left).

*I*n spite of the rocky, barren
nature of the countryside
around the village, abundant
sunshine and years of careful
irrigation still ensure that the stones
of the village are set off by splashes
of vegetation (this page *and*
opposite below).

This simple shrine (far left) is attached to the side of a village house; more elaborate, though dedicated to the same beliefs, is the furnishing of the parish church (left).

El Palmar VALENCIA

LIFE IN THE WETLANDS south of Valencia still draws on many age-old traditions, in spite of the presence of the Costa Blanca's high-rise hotels strung out along the skyline to form an incongruous backdrop to the east. This is the Albufera: 18,000 hectares of reedy marshland, its unique, largely freshwater lagoon is now protected and so able to sustain a variety of traditional human uses. Eel fishermen manœuvre along the narrow channels, often in traditional sailing boats; in season the wildfowlers come to shoot; and the finest rice in Spain is grown in the traditional manner in the paddy fields. One-hundred-metre-square plots are separated by miniature sea-walls, built to only a brick's thickness, which makes the progress of the often barefoot farmers along them look precarious to the point of foolhardiness, until it becomes apparent that the water within them is only inches deep. In these *arrozales*, a particularly prized variety of rice is grown, as it has been since the thirteenth century.

Floating on this orderly pattern of flooded squares is El Palmar itself, only four streets wide but many blocks in length, rather like the spine of a folding chess-board. Along its length on either side run small canals, in which are moored dozens of small fishing boats, exact replicas of the Venetian *sandale* – this being a lagoon after all. Every inhabitant seems to be a farmer, a fisherman or a chef – with good reason, as every weekend sees a huge motorized pilgrimage of gastronomes from the city. After a journey along the narrow dyke-top lanes and across even narrower bridges, negotiated with variable amounts of patience, the Valencianos can sit down in one of a dozen rival restaurants and pay homage to that inspired local invention, *paella*.

Treading in the footsteps of his forebears, a farmer tends his rice crops, repeating a process which dates from the thirteenth century. The rice fields, arrozales, *are separated from each other by narrow walls.*

Although El Palmar is often animated by visitors to its famous paella *restaurants, the* rías *which run parallel to its main street do provide havens of quiet (above left, above and* opposite*). And there is always the possibility of using unmotorized transport around the many lanes which criss-cross the lagoon (left).*

Montblanc

TARRAGONA

Defensive walls were first built around Montblanc in the fourteenth century; two-thirds of these are still standing today (opposite). *In the ancient centre of the village, at the top of the small hill around which the community first grew, the Plaça Mayor* (below) *lies peacefully in the shadow of the church.*

MONTBLANC'S ascent to fortune began during the reign of King Alfonso I, who in 1163 ordered it to be settled, under the rule of Pere Berenguer de Vilafranca. The site, by the banks of the river Francolí, was chosen for the defensive possibilities offered by a small hill, the Plá de Santa Barbara, on which was accordingly built a castle. The hill is still there, with the castle's remains on the top, just above the village's first church, which was dedicated to Santa María. Two centuries later the village, having made the best of its now ducal status and continuing royal favour, had long outgrown the old castle, and was in a position to demonstrate its prestige by building an encircling *muralla,* which remarkably is still completely intact today. This has over the years protected the labyrinth of ancient, winding streets within, which repay much exploration.

Between Santa María, still the main parish church, rebuilt during the prosperous years in a sumptuous Gothic style, and the nearby Romanesque church of San Miguel, lies the extensive Jewish quarter. It was not uncommon, in a mercantile community such as this, for the Moriscos and Jews to outnumber the indigenous population, at least until the Reconquista. Such heights of prosperity were not to be sustained for long, however, and Montblanc's fortunes diminished from the fifteenth century onwards, with a brief respite when vineyards brought some prosperity in the eighteenth century, before they were devastated by phylloxera in 1893.

According to Catalan legend, this is the very place where St. George slew his dragon, hence his position as Montblanc's patron saint. So he remained until 1867, when he was replaced in this role by San Matias, after a promise was made to that saint during a severe epidemic. Still, it is on St. George's Day each April that the villagers choose to celebrate their forebears' glorious past by dressing up in costumes for a week of feasting and medieval roistering, with re-enacted dragon-slaying.

*T*he walls of Montblanc are never far from sight (above), *an
ever-present reassurance for the village in times gone by.
Beneath them lie secret, quiet corners full of fascinating detail: a
flight of steps leading from the Plaça Mayor towards the church of
Santa María* (right)*; a portcullis still guards the Portal de San
Tordi* (above right)*. Suggestive of a prosperous past, grand
buildings abound in Montblanc: monumental stonework around
the church of Santa María* (opposite below), *and a stylish mansion
on the Plaça Mayor* (opposite above).

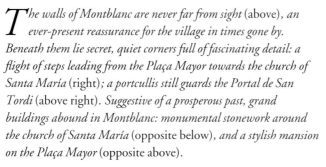

Peñíscola

CASTELLÓN

Within the ramparts (opposite), built in the time of Philip II, huddle the narrow streets and alleys of old Peñíscola, now free from motorized traffic: the Calle Castillo (below), off the Calle Santa Barbara and the Calle San Vicente (overleaf).

THE ROCKY HEADLAND that juts out into the Mediterranean from the sandy beaches of the Costa del Azahar had obvious attractions for the very earliest inhabitants of this stretch of coast: three freshwater springs and an easily defended position. A succession of Phoenician, Greek and Roman seafarers found in Peñíscola a secure base for coastal trade and for controlling the activities of rival shipping in the area from the original harbour to the north of the village.

It was the Knights Templar who, not many years after the departure of the Moorish rulers, built the present castle at the end of the thirteenth century. The massive gatehouse, which forms its only entrance, is emblazoned with the heraldic devices of the order, and of the Grand Master, Friar Berenguer de Cardona. Their tenure was short-lived, as the order was abolished a few years later. In 1411, the castle became a palace and Peñíscola a pontifical see, no less, after the arrival of the Aragonese Pedro de Luna, who had declared himself Pope Benedict XIII with the intention of unifying the Catholic world under his

control. His obdurate attempts to hang on to his title from his castle stronghold earned him the respect at least of his fellow Aragonese. 'Papa Luna' as they called him, lasted into his nineties, still professing a stalwart faith in his own supremacy.

Peñíscola underwent some serious tests of its defensive capabilities in the early nineteenth century, with the population suffering terrible losses in the closing months of the War of Independence, after a last bitter siege by Bourbon troops, in which sixty thousand cannon shots were fired. Nowadays, not a dent can be seen in the huge walls which, like the castle, have been restored to former splendour. Peñíscola is now besieged by holiday-makers, who gravitate here in great numbers to seek a day's respite from the cultural limitations of the other coastal resorts. The views of sea and coast from the ramparts are magical, but any attempts at recalling the romance of bygone ages are quickly thwarted by the determined efforts of local souvenir sellers, who make the already narrow streets almost impassable with their stalls.

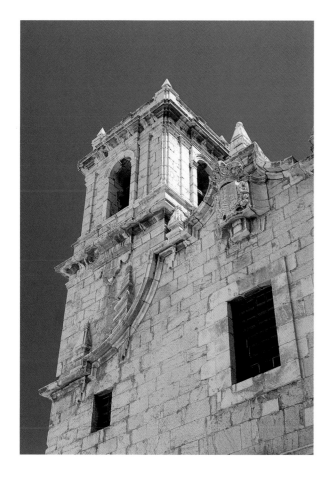

*T*he balconied streets by the Plaza Blas Perez (left *and* opposite) *and the venerable church of Nostra Señora de Ermitana* (above left) *are peaceful enough, but reminders of Peñiscola's troubled past are never far away in the form of the old battlements* (above).

*V iewed from the south (left), the village leaves no
doubt that it was intended as a substantial
stronghold; from its encircling ramparts to the mighty
stone castle (much restored) at its summit, Peñíscola's
whole aspect is defensive. On either side of the
promontory lie the developments of a more modern
resort, seen here from the Fortín del Bonete (above).*

Rupit BARCELONA

RUPIT is hidden deep in the woods in the far reaches of the province of Barcelona. Although that city is less than a hundred kilometres distant, its manic sprawl seems a world away from the timeless simplicity of this tiny village. After a long and winding drive, it is a relief to park the car and enter the village across a suspension footbridge, leading to a single stone-paved street which follows the curving course of the stream. The street, gradually narrowing, leads to the church, which is very easy to miss; from further away, however, it is easily identifiable by its prominent hexagonal bell-tower.

Past the church, lies the tiny Plaza Mayor, with balconied stone houses, and another, even smaller square which leads nowhere. An unobtrusive turning beside the church, however, becomes the Carrer del Fossar, which runs along the very spine of the village as it climbs irregularly up from the valley. This cobbled incline becomes a staircase, which in turn leads to the Plaza Cavaliers, which provides an opportunity to recover one's breath and enjoy the views over the wooded countryside. Hidden among the trees and accessible on one of the many pleasant woodland walks that are signposted from the village are the remains of several ancient chapels; closer at hand and visible from the Plaza, is the recently restored hermitage of Santa Magdalena.

Rupit may appear the epitome of peaceful isolation, but a stroll through the woods in the opposite direction will reach its anagrammatic neighbour, Pruit, with which it is twinned to form an administrative district. This stands proud but alone on top of a neighbouring crest, consisting only of a stately but under-used church, with matching hexagonal tower, a cemetery, and a single farmhouse.

*F*rom the main street of the village, which closely *follows the course of the tiny river Rupit and where most of the principal buildings are located, the stepped Carrer del Fossar winds uphill beside the parish church.*

*T*he village church (opposite), dedicated to St. Michael the Archangel, dates from the thirteenth century; the handsome octagonal bell-tower was added much later, in the late eighteenth century. A first-floor balcony on the Carrer de l'Eglesia looks well stocked with the utensils of rural living, including a rope and basket hoist (above). On the Carrer del Fossar, old sunlit stone is further illuminated by flowers in bloom (far left *and* left).

*I*n the sun, the village becomes a play of light and shade, the latter often provided by deeply recessed balconies and overhanging eaves (above), or the top-floor loggias of the older houses (right).

*I*n spite of its royal associations as the birthplace of Ferdinand of Aragón in 1452 and the subsequent belated addition of its regal suffix in the twentieth century, the village of Sos has kept its architectural treasures pretty much to itself. Its narrow streets are lined with unexpectedly fine houses (left); fine carving embellishes the entrance to the church of Sant'Esteban (above); and everything is capped in the time-honoured terracotta of the pantile roofs (opposite).

Sos del Rey Católico

ZARAGOZA

THE REGAL TITLE of this ancient hilltop village was actually granted in the 1920s, to celebrate belatedly the fact that Ferdinand, heir to the throne of Aragón, was born here in 1452. The crown prince spent little time in his birthplace, however, before setting off towards his glorious destiny as co-ruler, with Isabel of Castilla, of an almost unified Spain. But he was indeed born here, behind the impressive, emblazoned portals of the Palacio de los Sada, which can be discovered, with some difficulty, among the narrow medieval streets below the Plaza Mayor.

The village is surrounded by a stout wall, as befits the most important among a string of fortified outposts along the border with Navarra. There are a number of gates by which the visitor can begin exploring; none of them offers the guarantee of not getting lost en route to the citadel at the top, but they

do offer either a short, steep climb, or a longer, less breathless approach to the citadel. Here there is a keep and a fortified esplanade, with fine views as a reward for the climb. Surprisingly, the main church of the place, Sant'Esteban, which might by virtue of its importance and sheer size be expected to be prominently visible from the citadel, seems to have disappeared. This mystery is explained after a wander through a series of sunken, vaulted passageways which lead unexpectedly to the striking Romanesque main doorway: the village and its later fortifications are built up above the level of the church, which thus seems almost to have disappeared into the hill itself, despite the cathedral-like proportions of its interior. Further into the hill, and further back into the history of the village, is a small door leading from the nave to spiral stairs to the eleventh-century crypt.

*V*iewed from the grounds of the nearby chapel of Santa
Lucía, Sos del Rey climbs up its hill towards the citadel at
its summit (left). In the narrow streets which lead upwards,
stone and wood have acquired the patinas and textures of great
age and constant weathering (above).

ANDALUCÍA

*T*he produce of sun and irrigation methods originally perfected by Muslim settlers, the fruits of Andalucía include the extensive orange groves of Grazalema (above) and, more surprisingly, extensive vineyards (opposite), from which rises the little town of Montilla, near Córdoba.

TO DESCRIBE ANY REGION OF SPAIN as proudly independent is a truism: it is impossible to find one where the people do not feel that they are apart and in a large measure special. But in the southern part of Spain, the intensity of this feeling is something else again. The unique identity of this huge and varied area is expressed in the single name which covers the huge, rich valley of the Guadalquivir, the high Sierra Nevada and the sun-bathed coast, a name which evokes powerfully its Arab roots – Andalucía. It was a great triumph for the Reyes Católicos in 1492, when the beaten caliph Boabdil handed back the keys of Granada. With them went the last vestiges of Moorish political control, but the Christian Reconquista was unable to efface the culture that the Muslim occupiers had left behind them. Signs of their reign are everywhere in Spain, but here, where they settled for 600 years, and especially among the whitewashed, cubic houses of the Andalucían hill-villages, it often seems as though the subsequent centuries have laid down only a thin veneer of Europeanness. Yet this land is still essentially Spain. Here, the visitor feels not the dusty heat of Morocco, so close at hand as to be visible over the Straits of Gibraltar: just the warmest sun, the lushest of gardens, watered by trickling fountains, that so inspired the poets of al-Andalus.

*A*lmonaster la Real enjoys a secluded location in the wooded hill country of western Andalucía, close to the border with Portugal.

Alcalá la Real

JAÉN

OF ALL THE MOORISH STRONGHOLDS of Granada, Alcalá is the most majestic. Like the neighbouring forts at Alcaudete and Locubín, it was part of a vital protective barrier that separated the Christian world from the last strongholds of the Moors, especially Granada, fifty kilometres to the south, at the very heart of al-Andalus. Defending the fertile valley of the Guadalquivir as well as the northern approaches to Granada, Alcalá controlled both. Because of its strategic significance, the Moors took care to hold on to it, and retained it for a full six hundred years. In their defensive efforts they were aided by the natural advantages of its position on a high bluff, whose steepness can strike even today's visitor as monumental.

At the foot of the southern slope, the main street leads into the shady Paseo de los Alamos, where the old men of the village sit, stroll and dispute the issues of the day. For the visitor intent on gaining 'La Mota', as the citadel is known, there is a long and breathless climb from here to the outer gates of the fortress. As the ascent progresses, the streets are seemingly of increasing antiquity, and the style of the houses ages commensurately – by the time one pauses for breath by the venerable church of San Juan just below the fortress walls, the architecture is almost back to the simple white cube, reminiscent of the village houses of north Africa.

Entrance to the fortress itself is eventually gained through no less than three gatehouses and the imaginary gauntlet of whatever defenders of times past could think of hurling down from the ramparts above into the narrow, claustrophobic defiles between them. Three towers make up the fortress itself; these enclose a central courtyard, protected by a massive keep. Below this, excavations have uncovered the extraordinary extent of the settlement at the top of the lofty but secure plateau. This must have been a crowded little town, seething with life and activity, to judge by the extensive remains that archaeological diggings have revealed. Now it has a quiet, spacious aspect, with the sixteenth-century church of Santa María la Mayor looking out over a wide and empty plateau. Inside, more diggings have revealed the great antiquity of the place; where one would expect to see the nave, there is a maze of trenches that shows the legacy of previous inhabitants, including the remains of the first Gothic church and, below that, Roman tombs and two wells.

After many centuries of uninterrupted Moorish occupation, the twelfth century saw the fortress change hands several times. It was eventually recaptured in 1341, by the Christian forces under Alfonso XI. It was from here that the victorious Ferdinand and Isabel rode out to receive from a defeated caliph the keys to their final goal: Granada.

The tiny church of San Juan (above) *sits close to the summit of the hill crowned by the massive fortress of 'La Mota', a Moorish strongpoint for almost six hundred years. From the citadel the village unfolds towards the east* (opposite).

*T*ime present and time past both seem to move at a leisurely
pace in Alcalá. Matters of the day are discussed
at a mid-morning gathering on the Paseo de los Alamos
(opposite). A long and distinguished past makes itself felt,
remarkably, in the Roman remains excavated and exposed in
the nave of the abbey church (above left), which stands within
the fortress walls. The latter are reached by a steep climb (left)
towards the first of three fortified gatehouses. Visible
foundations within the fortifications reveal the extent of the
ancient settlement (above).

Almonaster la Real

HUELVA

A SURPRISING REGION, even for those accustomed to
the variety of Andalucía's countryside, is the
hinterland north of Huelva. This unfrequented and
peaceful area is reached by travelling inland from the
region's most western coast, north towards the border
with Portugal. After much twisting and turning, with
progressively more dramatic views whenever it emerges
from the trees, the road approaches the foothills of the
Sierra de Aracena. Despite their altitude, the hills are
well wooded, their climate mild beneath a covering of
chestnut, oak and cork trees. It is a very green picture,
quite unlike the arid bareness of other sierras, which
makes it all the more striking to turn a corner and
there discover a white village sitting on a hill.

This is Almonaster la Real, called 'al-Munastyr' by
the Arabs, who built their mosque over a Roman
monasterium, which itself had been built on the
remains of a Visigoth temple. A steep path from the
edge of the village leads steeply uphill to the site of this
architectural recycling, a climb worth doing because a
surprise is in store: the mosque has been miraculously
preserved, a thousand-year-old treasure. Beside it is
another curiosity, an enclosed bull-ring, one of two in
the vicinity, this one built in the nineteenth century,
using the remains of the ancient citadel.

In the quiet of the village below, the charming
parish church is much more easily to hand, built in the
Mudéjar style and dedicated to San Martín. The main
square nearby, the Plaza del Llano, is spacious and
open, but seems less of a centre to Almonaster than the
smaller, shady Plaza Constitución, which is wedged in
between the rather grand town hall and the small
Ermita de la Trinidad. Here, the apparent spell of
centuries-old quiet is broken for a moment, when
roller-skating children, released from school, career
around a small fountain, while old men on benches
prolong their siesta.

*Located on a site with plentiful supplies of wood and
water, Almonaster has been settled by a succession of
peoples and cultures from the early Bronze Age. The
remaining relics of successive generations include a castle,
a mosque, a hermitage and a bull-ring.*

*C*losed shutters and an absence of pedestrians give the *Plaza San Cristobal* (above) *an odd air of film-set stillness. Along it lies the parish church, dedicated to San Martín; its main door* (above right) *is a fine example of sixteenth-century Manueline design, a sign of significant Portuguese influence. Before the church was built in the village, the community made use of the mosque* (right) *left by the Moors on the site of the citadel. Its interior, complete with* mihrab, *has been well preserved. Another place of worship is the exquisite eighteenth-century chapel of La Trinidad on the tree-lined Constitucíon* (opposite).

Capileira GRANADA

THE CITY OF GRANADA is so central a destination for the visitor that it is a surprise to discover how close it lies, on the map at least, to one of the most obscure and disregarded regions in the whole of Spain. On the ground, the journey south-east to the mountainous region of the Sierra Nevada is, even on today's improved roads, a laborious undertaking. An ideal hideaway for refugees, the area was settled in the sixteenth century by the Moriscos – people of Arab descent who did not wish to leave Spain and who resisted the stern edicts of Philip II forbidding their language and traditional dress. Isolated from the rest of Spain, where Christianity was becoming rapidly re-established, they organized themselves into a rebellious army. One uprising was put down by Philip's forces in 1571, but unrest continued until 1609, when all the Moriscos were expelled from Spain. The terraced fields and orchards, separated by dry-stone walls which climb artfully up the steep slopes between the villages, are testament to the hard work and skill of these people. Despite its altitude, close to 1,500 metres, this has been a fertile area, as suggested by the Arab word *albasharat* (pasture-land), from which the villages' collective name, Las Alpujarras, is derived.

The villages themselves exhibit all the individual personality that might be expected from their long history and isolated position, most particularly in their similarity to their counterparts in the Atlas Mountains of north Africa. This is especially so of the decorative string of Capileira, Bubión and Pampaneira, which tumble headlong along the gorge of the ravine of El Baranco de Poqueira. Their cubic, whitewashed houses seem almost stuck to each other, built very close to provide a safe foothold on the steep slopes along which the villages lay. The narrow streets are often more like staircases. In Capileira, the fine Mudéjar church of Nuestra Señora de la Cabeza houses a polychrome statue of that name donated by the Reyes Católicos. This is brought out and celebrated in a procession on the last Sunday of April, while a more strenuous pilgrimage sets off on 5 August, along the road up out of the village, which winds the eleven kilometres up to the 3,400-metre Pico Veleta.

Three of the most interesting villages of Las Alpujarras lie strung out along the valley of the Poqueira. The climb up from the foot of this ravine first reveals Pampaneira, then Bubión (above)*, then finally Capileira, seemingly pushed up against the clouds* (opposite).

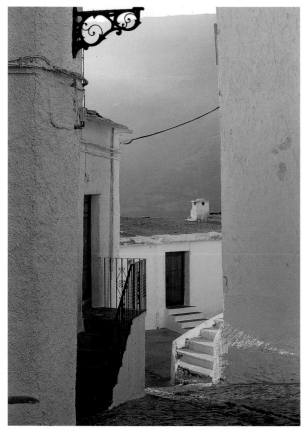

*T*he houses of the village cling cheek-by-jowl to one
another on the steeply sloping streets (above).
A relief for tired legs is offered by the flat expanse of the
Plaza Calvario (right), here the scene of a costumed
stand-off between the village children, a prelude to the
pre-Lent carnaval.

Grazalema
CÁDIZ

THE ANIMATED DAILY SCENE in Grazalema's main square, overlooked by its smart town hall, gives little indication that this tranquil mountain village has seen more than its share of ill fortune. The Moors thought it important enough to be fortified, lying as it does on the frontier of the caliphate of Granada. They called it Ben-Zalema, and it became Gran-Zalema before their defeat in 1485 by Rodrigo Ponce de León, duke of Arcos.

Once more in Christian hands, its rise to prosperity was such that by the eighteenth century it could boast four churches and ten thousand inhabitants. Its farmers had done very well, as had the small-scale weaving industry, producing blankets from the local wool. Bands of brigands were a problem, the sierras providing the ideal terrain for evading the authorities, of which there were few. Later, Napoleon's armies brought devastation to the place; they left a weakened and depopulated community without the means to defend itself. Reports from the latter part of the nineteenth century tell a sorry tale of villagers at the mercy of bandits, murderous secret societies, and anarchist bands of disaffected workers. The Civil War and its aftermath also hit Grazalema badly, as it did so many of the rural communities of Andalucía, which were left with no work and very little food.

The population has recovered gradually during the last thirty years or so; tourism has also come to the rescue, attracting huge numbers annually to the Costa del Sol, some of whom are then persuaded to tour the famous White Villages of Andalucía and the surrounding mountains. There has even been a resurgence in demand for the traditional blankets, keeping the old hand looms busy in a number of the village houses. Few summer visitors, admiring the sparkling whiteness of its pretty old houses, would guess that they are standing in the wettest place in Spain. Humid air blowing in from the Atlantic through the Bay of Cádiz, funnels up to Grazalema where it meets its first serious mountains. The resultant downpours give Grazalema a rainfall of twice the national average for Spain and six times the average for Andalucía.

The parish church of San José rises majestically from the centre of the village against the backdrop of the surrounding sierra (opposite). *In the main square* (above) *the fountain heads seem to be oddly concerned with the content of the very serious conversation taking place in the foreground.*

*T*he surrounding hills are scarcely ever out of sight on the
sloping streets of Grazalema (above). Such is the sloping
of the village streets that church towers and roofs always seem at
an angle to each other (above right *and* right). Houses of great
elegance line the steep climb of the Calle Mateos Galgo towards
the church of San José (opposite).

Medina Sidonia CÁDIZ

*T*he character of Medina is defined by the conjunction of Islam and Christianity, dual themes which run everywhere in the village. There is also a modern quarter, reached by a reminder of the place's Moorish past in the form of the Arco de la Pastora (the Shepherdess's Gate) which pierces the ancient walls (opposite). *A classical doorway* (above) *lends an imposing note to the otherwise modest church of Santiago el Mayor.*

SIGHTING MEDINA SIDONIA from afar, across the fertile Barbate plain, it is easy to pick out the Torre de Doña Blanca, the tall tower next to the imposing church of Santa María la Mayor. But Medina's importance, due in a large part to its position on the plain, goes back many centuries before the building of the church in the fifteenth century. Even when neighbouring Cádiz was still establishing itself (and most historians are happy to allow Cádiz its claim to be called Europe's oldest city), Medina was already the centre of a Phoenician colony that supplied the growing port with its agricultural goods. In one of the little streets not far from the summit of the village, an extensive network of sewers and watercourses has recently been uncovered, the scale of which leaves no doubt that this was also an important centre under the Roman occupation as well.

Medina later came under the control of the influential dukes of the Guzmán family, to whom King Juan II gave the duchy of Medina Sidonia in

1472. As the status of the place and the wealth derived from the rich farmlands around grew, so churches and convents were built. Many of the finest buildings survive, and a climb up to the pleasantly deserted highest point will reveal remains of both a Visigothic fortress and a later Christian castle, which look down over a number of handsome seventeenth- and eighteenth-century mansions.

Right beside the cloister of the grandiose parish church, stands the Convento de Jesús, María y José, whose nuns became known as *las Monjas de arriba*, to distinguish them from their sisters of the Convento San Cristóbal down the hill (*las Monjas de abajo*). Still further down, the ancient walls facing the modern town to the north-west are pierced by the most perfect reminder of Medina's Moorish past, the Arco de la Pastora, or Shepherdess's Gate. Below the horseshoe arch a steep stairway leads out of the ancient quarter and back to the present-day realities of the village's main street.

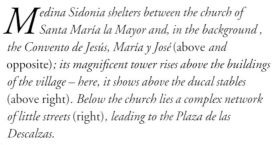
*M*edina Sidonia shelters between the church of
Santa María la Mayor and, in the background ,
the Convento de Jesús, María y José (above *and*
opposite); *its magnificent tower rises above the buildings
of the village – here, it shows above the ducal stables*
(above right). *Below the church lies a complex network
of little streets* (right), *leading to the Plaza de las
Descalzas.*

Moguer HUELVA

LIMOSNA

*I ronically, the flowers in this deliberate arrangement
around a wall shrine (above) are artificial, while those
springing unscripted from the tower of Nostra Señora de la
Granada (opposite) are undoubtedly real – an impromptu
addition to the already highly decorated eighteenth-century
Seville Baroque of the church.*

THE RÍO TINTO, famous for the mineral deposits
extracted from it since Roman times, flows out into
the Gulf of Cádiz amid a gently rolling countryside,
lightly dotted with strawberry fields, olive groves and
vineyards. Moguer, the port nearest to the sea on its
banks, might have remained a quiet fishing village if it
had not been for the efforts of the ruling Portocarrero
family to establish a more serious maritime reputation.
Their forbear, Alfonso Jofre Tenorio, had been
granted the village with its surrounding land by King
Alfonso XI, whom he had served as admiral.

The early fifteenth century was a propitious time to
speculate on the expansion of shipping; shipyards were
being established at Moguer, and skilled craftsmen
arrived to swell a population already consisting of a
good number of experienced seamen. It was to this
hive of shipping activity that Christopher Columbus
came several times while he was looking for support
for his audacious scheme to cross the Atlantic. Here he
found not only the shipbuilding and chandlering
expertise that he was looking for, but also a
noblewoman who was to prove extremely helpful. She
was Doña Iñes Enriques, abbess of the community of
Santa Clara, and a kinswoman of King Ferdinand.
After a helpful word from her, Moguer received the
royal decree on 30 April 1492, ordering the
construction and fitting out of *tres carabelas armadas y
equipadas* ('three armed and equipped caravels'), in
which the explorer duly set sail; more than half his
crew came from Moguer.

Their seamanship and the stoutness of his own
vessel, the *Niña*, did not fail Columbus in his epic
voyage, and on his triumphant return he gave thanks
at Santa Clara; the elegant church and cloister of the
convent still stand near the centre of the village,
among peaceful streets of whitewashed houses. In one
of these, the Calle de la Ribera, the poet Juan Ramón
Jiménez was born in 1881. Even during the painful
years of his long American exile during the Franco era,
and despite the international fame that earned him the
Nobel Prize for Literature, these streets that he called
'un paraíso de luz' still inspired his poetry and his
memories of the Andalucía of his youth.

*T*he presence of the locally born Nobel laureate poet,
Juan Ramón Jiménez, is everywhere in Moguer: in
the elegant street which bears his name (opposite) *and in
the Plaza Cabildo in the form of a substantial statue*
(left). *A certain secretive quality of life is suggested by
shutters and window grilles on the Calle Reyes Católicos,
seen from the loggia of the town-hall, and the forbidding
entrance to the religious community of Santa Clara on the
Plaza de las Monjas* (above).

Andalucía · 103

*M*any of Moguer's houses display a restrained
elegance: wrought-iron balconies combine
beautifully with classical door and windows (above).
The prosperity which these private residences express is
confirmed by the substantial look of Moguer (right),
surrounded by wine-producing country and at the centre
of the largest strawberry-producing region in Spain.

Sanlúcar de Barrameda

CÁDIZ

The legacy of Spain's Moorish civilization is clearly visible in the external detailing of the nineteenth-century Palacio de Orleans y Borbón (above), now the local ayuntamiento (town-hall). Narrow lanes, lined with fine houses, lead from the Plaza de la Paz towards Nostra Señora de la Caridad, which shows itself in the form of its bell-tower above the neighbouring roofs (opposite).

ITS POSITION at the mouth of the Guadalquivir river made Sanlúcar de Barrameda the natural chief port for Seville, fifty kilometres upstream. The place's fame (Magellan set off from here on his circumnavigation of the globe) and prosperity increased with the volume of trade, especially after the riches started to stream back from the New World. Its prestige was further enhanced during the nineteenth century, when the fashion for spending the summer at the seaside caught on with the nobility of Seville. This novelty proved understandably popular as, although it is not far inland, that city can swelter for weeks at temperatures in the mid thirties.

All the facilities for patrician ease are to be found here: graceful tree-lined avenues for the evening *paseo*, a theatre and a conservatoire of music, and a splendid beach whose flat sands have inspired a further diversion in the form of a horse race, still held every August. Exploration of the warren of streets in the old centre will discover many painted *palacios* still bearing the names of their noble owners. In the fishermen's quarter of Bajo de Guía, excellent seafood restaurants

face the beach. Further along the shore, another district, Bonanza, lives up to its name every afternoon, when fishing boats converge on the small dock to unload their catch, which immediately becomes the subject of a fast and furious auction.

Sanlúcar's benign climate has inspired another great source of pride: the local sherry produced in the cathedral-sized *bodegas* on the hill above the village. The rarest of microclimates, a combination of the cooling sea-breezes and plenty of oxygen (hence the size of the *bodegas*), allows the formation of a 'veil of yeast' which sits on the surface of the wine and reduces oxidization during the long months of its maturation. The result is the driest and un-tawniest of sherries, as refreshing as can be desired. Called *manzanilla*, after the camomile – pale straw-yellow tinged with green – it resembles, it has the great distinction of being the chosen drink of Seville's mighty April Feria. The high regard in which it is held and the pride of Sanlúcar in producing it inspire its own celebration every May, when the Sanluqueños and Sanluqueñas dance for a week during their own Feria de la Manzanilla.

A striking feature of Sanlúcar's old quarter is the quantity of elegant merchants' houses, a testament to a prosperous past and a pretty enjoyable present as a summer resort for the inhabitants of Seville (this page). The standing of the place is somehow evident in the formal façades of this row of houses (opposite) in the Calle Luis Equilas, leading to the grand church of Nuestra Señora de la O.

Overleaf
*T*he central square of Sanlúcar (p. 110), the Plaza de Cabildo, is the scene of many of the festivities celebrated by the Sanluqueños. Another favourite meeting place in the former parade ground, the Calzada del Ejército, surrounded by pleasant arcades (p. 111).

Vejer de la Frontera CÁDIZ

An ornate fountain, complete with sculpted frogs, adorns the tiny Plaza de España (opposite), just outside the old walls of the village. In contrast to the animation of the square are the narrow streets inside the walls, quiet and closed, suggesting the place's close relationship with the culture of the southern shores of the Mediterranean (below).

THE ANDALUCÍANS have recently chosen to name the stretch of coast that runs from the Portuguese border to Gibraltar the 'Costa de la Luz'. Certainly there is enough room on its spacious beaches to accommodate some overspill from the full-to-bursting resorts of the better-known Costa del Sol to the east, but apart from those, the coastline is uneventful. 'Luz' there is in plenty, however, and few sights can rival the first glimpse of Vejer de la Frontera, glowing in its whiteness as it rises from the flat coastal plain.

The old village is still surrounded by its medieval walls; outside these a nineteenth-century promenade, the Corredera, provides room to stretch the legs and enjoy the view to the north, before the visitor plunges into the intricate and irregular layout of streets inside the walls. Here, glimpses of the outside world are more haphazard and unexpected, as the walls themselves follow the ups and downs of the rocky hill. Around a corner of the Convento de las Conceptionistas is one such unexpected view, framed by the Arco de las Monjas (Nuns' Gate), which separates the former Jewish quarter, standing in the shadow of the walls to the west, from the higher part of the village. Hiding near to the oldest gate of all, the tenth-century Arco de la Segur (Axe Gate), is the parish church of El Divino Salvador (Divine Saviour), built on top of the former mosque, and retaining its minaret. The Muslim occupiers also left behind a castle that they built in the eleventh century on the topmost point of the village. But most Moorish of all is the feeling that comes from wandering around the close labyrinth of winding streets. From these, the visitor may pop out unexpectedly through the Arco de la Villa, straight into the tiny tree-lined main square, the Plaza de España.

*T*he vertical lines of delicate wrought-iron balconies confer
a refined elegance on the façades of the houses in
the Calle Nuestra Señora de la Oliva (opposite). Much older
is the parish church of El Divino Salvador, which stands on the
site of a former mosque in the centre of the old quarter (this
page); a walk around its walls reveals a wealth of detail in
unexpected corners.

The whitewashed houses of Vejer's centre cling together in a way suggestive of a north African hill village; the one emphatic symbol of the Reconquista, the church, looks somehow like an intruder.

THE HEART OF SPAIN

A coat of arms on Almagro's Plaza Santo Domingo recalls the military and economic power of Castilla during Spain's Golden Age (above). This central region is also a place of endless plains, like those of La Mancha, made famous by the wanderings of Cervantes' Don Quixote and his encounters with windmills (opposite).

THE ANCIENT KINGDOM OF CASTILLA occupies the greater part of the inescapable geological feature that is, effectively, central Spain: the Meseta. This vast, elevated plateau of windswept plains, criss-crossed by jagged mountain ranges, has provided a dramatic setting for its storytellers, whose heroes, from El Cid to Don Quixote, have had to prove their mettle against the backdrop of its often harsh terrain. Its epic scale may prove equally daunting for today's visitor, too, despite a network of superb new highways. But to speed across these huge plains may be to miss the pleasures of slowing down to visit some of the wonderful historic villages that dot the landscape.

Scraping a living from this land was always a hard business, even at the best of times: Romans, Visigoths and Moors in their turn came here to subdue the countryside rather than to settle it. It is common to find the remains of their settlements perched defensively on some rocky outcrop. Despite the odds, however, some of the inhabitants managed to accumulate considerable wealth through the centuries; by medieval times, for instance, the wool fairs of Medina del Campo had grown to be the largest in Europe. This prosperity then suffered a period of decline during Spain's so-called Golden Age, when the rapacity of successive monarchs brought disaster to the Castillan economy through ever-greater demands for tax. The resulting depopulation of the whole region is only now being reversed, while its cultural treasures, which have become far more accessible, are playing a part in bringing back its prosperity.

*I*n the northernmost part of
Castilla large-scale farming on
the prairie undoubtedly flourishes,
but the communities have dwindled
in size, giving the place an even
greater air of desolation.

Almagro
CIUDAD REAL

A place of strikingly elaborate building, like the soaring façade of San Bartolomé, Almagro can reflect on its past eminence as the headquarters of the important military order of the Knights of Calatrava from the thirteenth century to the end of the fifteenth. The Plaza Mayor is colonnaded, with striking upper galleries of green-framed windows (opposite).

FOR THOSE TRAVELLERS who do not acquire a taste for the featureless flatlands of La Mancha, the road towards the riches of Andalucía in the south may be the main attraction of the region. But it is certainly worth pausing in Almagro, which sits quietly aloof from the main roads, in the centre of the huge Campo de Calatrava. Its grand old buildings tell of a rich history, since the first settlement grew up around an important Roman crossroads. After the centuries of Moorish domination of the area, under the caliphate of Córdoba, the Christian kings pushed south to reconquer the territory, capturing the castle of Calatrava in 1147. In this part of Spain they relied on the support of military-religious orders such as the Knights of Calatrava, granted a formal concession by Ferdinand III in 1222 to exploit a huge area from Malagon in the north, to Almuradiel in the south.

Almagro, lying midway, became their headquarters, eclipsing for a while Ciudad Real, now the capital town of the region. As well as developing the agriculture of the area (the renowned aubergines grown here today boast their own *Denominación de Origen*), the order also exploited the mines at nearby Almadén, funded by the eminent German merchant families, such as the Fuggers and the Wessels, who had moved to the area. The cultural as well as the commercial importance of Almagro during the succeeding centuries (there was even a university here from 1574 to 1828) is reflected in the network of streets around the stately Plaza Mayor. An excellent restoration programme has given the narrow streets, many of them cobbled, an attractive air of genteel familiarity, as they curve between whitewashed houses, churches and convents, many adorned with striking stone doorways carved with the arms and emblems of the orders and noble families.

The Plaza Mayor itself, originally laid out as a military parade ground, has twin colonnades running along its length, supporting long first-floor galleries whose green-framed decorative windows look out on the bustle below. In July, the promenading crowds may be gathering for a theatrical performance at the adjoining Corral de Comedias, a rare survival from the beginning of the seventeenth century – a courtyard theatre where travelling players once performed in front of a milling audience on the ground floor, while the nobility viewed proceedings from the comfort and shade of the balconies above.

122

*I*n the heart of Spain lie the villages of Castilla-La Mancha; this particular example (above) is close to the village of El Toboso, famous as the fictional home of Dulcinea, mistress of Don Quixote. And everywhere in La Mancha there is space and openness – here, just west of Almagro (opposite).

Calatañazor

SORIA

AFTER THREE HOURS' DRIVING north from Madrid, and still far short of the vineyards of La Rioja, the traveller may well feel trapped in time, hypnotized by the seemingly endless, dream-like plains of Castilla. The prospect of a return to reality, in the form of the comfortable provincial capital of Soria, causes most drivers to hurtle past a remarkable medieval gem: Calatañazor. A little side-road off the main highway curls around the *mesa* to reveal the dramatic sight of the village clustered around its castle on its own outcrop, dominating the plains beyond.

With hardly any visible signs of restoration, the village presents a character determinedly rooted in the past. Its cobbled streets are best explored on foot; there, old houses, shops and inns lean towards each other, supported by wooden pillars made from local savin trees. Latticeworks of branches hold together their ancient walls, filled with a random collection of materials – terracotta, adobe and, occasionally, brick.

The irregularly shaped main square holds two ancient symbols of the community – an elm tree, and a strange cylindrical pillar topped with a weather vane. From here, and from the ruined castle keep alongside, there is a commanding view of the fertile plain below. Peaceful and productive though it now appears, with only an occasional chugging tractor interrupting the stillness, the name of the place – El Valle de la Sangre (The Valley of Blood) – is a reminder of the mighty battle fought here a thousand years ago, at which the remarkable Muslim leader Abi amir Muhammad, who bore the title 'al-Mansur bi-Allah' ('victorious for Allah'), an able politician as well as a perpetual warmonger, who had dominated much of Castilla during his long reign, met his final defeat and death in 1002.

The village is dominated by the ruins of its medieval castle (opposite) *which overlooks the plain on which the Muslim troops of al-Mansur are said to have been defeated by Christian forces. Many of the remaining medieval houses are capped by oddly shaped conical chimneys* (left).

The stone paved streets and open spaces of Calatañazor are lined with ancient buildings which seem to grow into each other (this page). In the Plaza Mayor is one of those odd details which make a village immediately memorable: a strange cylindrical pillar topped by a weather vane (opposite).

Candelario

SALAMANCA

The streets of the village rise steeply (opposite) *from the Plaza Mayor* (below)*, where refreshment is provided by the 'El Dolar' café-bar.*

PERCHED ON ITS OWN SIERRA, at an altitude of 1,100 metres, the mountain village of Candelario occupies an isolated yet commanding position above the flat plains to east and south. It is in the southernmost tip of the province of Salamanca, and equally distant from the borders of Ávila and Cáceres. Evidence of medieval mining has been found near the village, and it could have been minerals that attracted the attention of the Roman occupiers of Castilla.

In later centuries, when not drawing wages in the military service of Alfonso VIII against the invading Moors, the villagers relied on their herds for survival – goats, ideally adapted for the high pastures, and increasingly, cattle and pigs. By the middle of the nineteenth century, according to records of the time, Candelario was raising a total of 8,000 pigs and 2,000 cattle each year, mostly to provide the ingredients for the famous local *chorizo* sausage, which was hand-made in more than a hundred workshops in the village. An even greater number of houses were in use for drying the meat before the sausages were made.

Several of the village houses are still set up with drying racks for the meat; many more have the three-storey configuration typical of these mountain villages. The ground floor housed the animals, while the human members of the family lived on the first floor and slept on the top floor, which typically had a balcony sheltered by a double set of eaves – the snowfall there being heavy and long-lasting.

The whole village is set on a steep slope, with church and town hall compressed towards the upper reaches, while the Plaza Mayor, with more space to spread itself, lies at the foot of the hill. Two main streets run down from the top gate to the square, both equally narrow and irregularly flagged, and laid out with a purposeful gully to help drain off the snowmelt. Many of the older houses have an additional half-door built against their ground-floor entrance as an extra layer of protection against flooding. A large number of outside house walls are clad with upturned roof-tiles – further evidence of the harsh winter winds that blow in over the high ground to the west.

*I*n the centre of the Plaza Mayor
stands the small chapel of the
Santísimo Cristo del Refugio
(above). *One interesting local
architectural curiosity is the*
batipuerta (right), *a sort of second
door to hold back the torrents
which can career alarmingly down
the steep cobbled streets when the
snow melts on the high mountains
which are such a visible presence
around the village* (opposite).

*F*rom the top of the village the view unfolds beyond a foreground of traditional pantile rooftops.

A local guide briefs visitors before they disappear into the vast monastic complex. The massive scale of the buildings completely dominates this staging-post for pilgrims, seen here (opposite) *from the road from Navalmoral to the north.*

The striking façade of the main church, golden in colour and with a mixture of Gothic and Moorish decoration, dominates the small main square of the village. Behind it, as the monastery grew in size and importance, an increasing number of buildings were crammed within the fortified walls. The visitor can now wander between the succeeding architectural styles of the monastery's heyday, from the elegant Mudéjar pavilion of 1405 to the sixteenth-century Gothic cloister, now part of the comfortable Hospedería del Real Monasterio.

No less inviting are the tiny streets that radiate out from the square, the oldest of which, the Calle Sevilla, winds under an arch, down between Renaissance houses, towards the tiny Plaza de los Tres Chorros, with its three-spouted fountain. Solemn processions trail through these streets each 8 September, as the villagers celebrate their patron saint, bearing her aloft on her bier. Inside the monastery, the holy figure herself can be viewed from the floor of the church, in its niche high above the main altar, or upstairs in its own octagonal sanctuary. Higher ranking pilgrims used to ascend to the first floor of the Treasury, where an intimate boudoir had been built on the other side of the altar wall. Here, in return for a suitable donation, a monk will still be happy to rotate the saint through 180 degrees for a face-to-face encounter. The little figure, dwarfed by gold trappings that contrast strangely with the age-darkened oak from which it is carved, looks almost older than its own religion. It became a powerful symbol of the Hispanidad, the world-wide Spanish-speaking community; a sizeable Mexican city and one of Columbus' Caribbean islands were given the name of the village. And it was to this church, in 1496, that Columbus himself bought two of his native American servants, to be baptized into the faith of their conquerors.

Guadalupe
CÁCERES

THIS VILLAGE IMPRESSES immediately, not because of its overall size, but by the scale of the monastic complex around which it huddles. It was a miraculous event in the early fourteenth century that was to bring fame and countless pilgrims to this secluded valley. A local shepherd is said to have experienced a vision of St. Mary which led him to discover a wooden effigy of the saint, hidden by the little river Guadalupe five centuries before, when the Moorish armies were overrunning the area. By the time of the effigy's recovery, the Reconquista was well under way, and the grateful king, Alfonso XI, founded a monastery on the spot following his victory over the Muslim armies at Salado in 1340.

Beneath the soaring towers and majestic façades of the Real Monasterio, facing on to the Plaza Santa María (below), Guadalupe soon resumes a more domestic scale in the Calle Sevilla. This delightful little street leads to the Plaza de los Tres Chorros, where the eponymous three spouts still disgorge mountain water into the fountain's basin (opposite).

Overleaf

Pilgrims still flock to the shrine of the Virgin of Guadalupe and, naturally, wish to bear away souvenirs of their visit – an urge which the local copper-smelting workshops are only too ready to satisfy (p. 140). Equally full of intricate detail as the souvenir shop window is the Gothic confection of the monastery church's west front (p. 141), oddly suggestive of the intense and concentrated decoration of Islamic architecture.

La Guardia TOLEDO

Simple yet quietly grand, the parish church (opposite and above) rises above the Plaza Mayor. Across the road, a sculpted coat of arms above the doorway of the Casa de los Jaenes proclaims it as one of the village's most prestigious dwellings (above right).

THE PLAINS OF TOLEDO lie not far to the south of Madrid. Lacking the surreal emptiness and huge expanse of La Mancha and smaller in scale, they are relieved by a series of rocky plateaux (*mesas*) which rear up dramatically from the flat floor of the valleys. Below one of the most imposing of these, the Mesa de Ocaña, runs the busy N-IV, bearing heavy traffic between Madrid and Andalucía. A little way south, it passes close to the small and ancient village of La Guardia, where the present-day inhabitants benefit from the defensive prudence of their medieval predecessors, who settled on top of a miniature *mesa*, protected on three sides by steep cliffs. So lofty is La Guardia's perch, that a stroll along the cliff-top promenades to enjoy the cooling breeze of a summer evening will not be disturbed by much more than a distant murmur from the traffic hurtling below.

Freed from defensive constraints, today's village is more accessible than in previous centuries; a viaduct leads over the gorge that separates the new parts from

the older centre. Despite this, a timeless air of repose still surrounds the narrow streets and the many venerable buildings which survive there. On one side of the leafy main square, the imposing parish church, built and added to during the seventeenth and eighteenth centuries, faces the Casa de los Jaenes, a grand mansion whose elaborately carved doorway proclaims its past importance as the house of a noble family. Round the corner is an equally distinguished building, the sixteenth-century synagogue, evidently spied on in times past by means of a peephole built into the wall of the neighbouring hermitage. Below the village ramparts, a network of cave dwellings has been carved out of the rock; residents used to dig further and further into the hill to accommodate each addition to their families. Further burrowing in the sixteenth century resulted in the tiny and fascinating Ermita del Santo Niño nearby; it has a simple nave and a variety of niches and side chapels carved out of the rock in pleasing irregularity.

The former owners of the Casa de los Jaenes (opposite) *obviously believed that they had something valuable to protect in the house. But La Guardia is largely a very open place, of sleepy promenades and bucolic rhythms* (above *and* right).

The Heart of Spain · 145

La Huetre CÁCERES

THERE IS A WILD AND RUGGED CORNER of Extremadura, tucked under the snow-capped sierras of Salamanca, and not far from the Portuguese border, which seems to be almost off the map of Spain. Apart from its relative inaccessibility (it is still an hour's determined driving from almost anywhere), it has long remained beyond the boundaries of most Spaniards' mental map of their own country, its very name (Las Hurdes) a byword for rural backwardness and deprivation. When the young Spanish film-maker Luis Buñuel read a documentary study of the area, written by the Frenchman Maurice Legendre, he was inspired by the extremes of poverty there to shoot his 1933 Surrealist film, which he called simply *Las Hurdes*. Equally direct was its title for overseas audiences: *Tierra sin Pan (Land without Bread)*.

Winding up and around the spectacular valleys of Las Hurdes, the road eventually comes to a stop at La Huetre, as far up the headwaters of the river Hurdano as it is possible to go by car. The village sits in an unlikely position, pinned against the sheer slopes of the sierra and bisected by a rushing torrent, while the little alleys scramble up and down between the slate and rubble cottages. To meet some of the older villagers here, many of them bent by years of toil, is to realize the grim truth about the surrounding countryside: though unspoilt and spectacularly beautiful, it has been an ungenerous land. Even for the agile goats of the district, the pickings are slim. The local bees have an easier time, however, producing their excellent honey from the wild mountain flowers and from the fruit orchards that form a colourful patchwork along the valleys in spring.

It looks idyllic in the sun, spread across its mountainside, but in fact the inhabitants of this land were traditionally among the poorest in Spain. Times have changed, though, since Luis Buñuel made his film about the hardships of the people (Las Hurdes) *and the influx of European money is bringing a degree of prosperity to the region.*

*G*oats are returned to the village after the morning grazing (opposite); *this is still an entirely agricultural economy dependent on the hard living which the land grudgingly provides. The simplicity of the houses* (this page) *is indicative of a society with few pretensions; mains water and electricity arrived here later than anywhere else in Spain.*

Overleaf
*T*he building materials in La Huetre look scarcely *distinguishable from the surrounding rock – from which they have undoubtedly been taken. The stonework is as rough as the very earth of the village's setting.*

Pedraza SEGOVIA

THE VERY FIRST SIGHTING of this hilltop village leaves no doubt that it is a place of some consequence. The imposing Puerta de la Villa, reinforced by the medieval gaol next door, gives a conditional welcome (this being the only entrance to the place and the only exit) to those who have toiled up a curving ramp to enter the village beneath a lively brickwork frieze and venerable coat of arms. This last belongs to the Valasco family, the dukes of Frías, who were feudal overlords here for four centuries. During this time, the rich pasturage in this corner of Segovia's province brought wealth to them, as well as to the local wool merchants. The village was once noisy with a profusion of workshops, where the wool was processed before going to the market – all silent now, although excellent roast lamb still tops the bill of fare in the village's several restaurants.

Narrow streets curve up from the Puerta, between fine stone houses (some emblazoned with more coats of arms) towards the Plaza Mayor, a grand square in miniature, with carved stone pillars supporting balconies over its galleried arcades. There is nothing small-scale about Pedraza's castle, once the seat of the Valasco family, which huddles massively at the western end of the high rocky escarpment. Solid gate-towers still flank a fearsomely studded door, but there is no longer anything to protect, other than the antiques collection of its last seigneur, the realist painter Ignacio Zuloaga, who bought the property in 1926.

As the village population has dwindled during the centuries since its wool-rich heyday, the tidemark of houses has receded from the castle's rather forbidding façade towards the old centre, around the Plaza Mayor and the church of Santa María, one of four churches that served the needs of the community in busier times. The resulting expanse of empty ground, with its commanding views, has a wistful spaciousness that complements pleasantly Pedraza's air of past importance and impregnability.

As much today as in the days of the warring counts of Segovia, Pedraza has the air of a powerful stronghold. High on its rocky bluff, still surrounded by defensive walls and watchtowers, the village can only be approached by its original fortified gate, built into the old gaol, and seen here to the right of this view of the south-eastern approaches.

The Heart of Spain · 153

*O*ne of four churches which once served Pedraza's faithful, simple and powerful San Juan adjoins the nearby Plaza Mayor (opposite). *In the foreground is an ancient well-head – on the Plaza de la Olma. A water source of more recent use adorns a corner of the Calle de la Cordovilla. Detailing within the village varies from the sinister spiking of a door in the castle keep* (far left) *to the display of the morning's bread in the local bakery* (left).

*G*enerally agreed to be one of the prettiest squares in the whole of Spain, the Plaza Mayor is lined with sixteenth-century houses, their first-floor balconies supported by quaintly irregular stone pillars (left). Away from the centre, houses are less intensely crowded together (below), while the castle (opposite) faces an expanse of empty ground, although this was covered with dwellings in Pedraza's heyday.

NORTHERN SPAIN

In north-eastern Spain the often harsh winter climate of the foothills of the Pyrenees has produced an architecture almost alpine in style, typified in the pronounced eaves and tiny windows of this house in Ituren (Navarra). Four kingdoms away, at the western extremity of northern Spain, near Ribadavia (Ourense) in Galicia, stands Beade's church of Santa María amid some of the most fruitful vineyards in Spain (opposite).

SPAIN IS A HUGE COUNTRY, and never feels more so than when the visitor who has become acclimatized to the south first experiences the north coast. Over the rocky coastline, the fierce Atlantic brings in plenty of rain, and a lush greenness colours the countryside that runs from the foothills of the Pyrenees to the rocky Cabo Finisterre in the far west. The Bay of Biscay was the tough training ground for the sailors of the Pais Vasco, the Basque country, whose seamanship, tested in whaling expeditions across the Atlantic, was to help make real Spanish dreams of imperial dominion in the far-off Americas. Not that this fiercely independent people, allied to their Basque cousins across the Pyrenees, were particularly interested in obliging the Castillan monarchs out of a sense of duty, and they never abandoned their ambitions of separation from a centralized Spain. Recent decentralization of the country's political structure has gone some way towards satisfying these ambitions (not far enough for the Basques), and it is true that, of all the separate regions in the north, self-government suits them very well.

The north of Spain has long been used to an influx of visitors, since the Middle Ages in fact, when the stream of pilgrims began to make its way westwards to the holy shrine of Santiago de Compostela. They had many churches to visit on the way – the Moors had little influence here, after their expulsion by the Asturian kings in the eighth century, and hardly made any impression on Galicia, which remained very much a land apart until the influx of holidaymakers in more recent times.

*O*nce again enjoying a degree of independence, the ancient kingdom of Navarra encompasses a wide range of terrains, from the barren plains south of Pamplona to alpine greenery on the approaches to the Pyrenees (right).

Bárcena Major CANTABRIA

As befits a village which has depended for its essential materials on the surrounding woodland since time immemorial, the inhabitants of Bárcena Mayor boast considerable expertise with axe, chisel and, occasionally, chainsaw (opposite). Roughcast stone houses (above), with characteristic deep eaves and wooden balconies, are held together by venerable timbers.

THE ROAD TO BÁRCENA MAYOR, winding purposefully through steep wooded valleys in this most secluded corner of Cantabria, turns out to have no further purpose after depositing the visitor within reach of the remote village. Indeed, it would scarcely be able to carry on, as the uneven cobbled streets that twist and turn between the old stone houses are far more suited to their usual traffic of cattle and the occasional tractor.

Cantabria's famously green countryside is largely dedicated to the happiness of its huge bovine population, and Bárcena is no exception. The land immediately round the village is both precipitous and thickly wooded, so the pastures higher up the valley are a significant commuting distance away. Accordingly, the herd stays up on the hill-top pastures from spring to early winter, and then returns to be boarded in the

village until May. This practice is not an idiosyncratic rarity: almost every house has its ground floor given over to the stalls, often with the original earth floor. As though to compensate for this inclusive attitude to cattle, the human quarters, which start on the floor above, are exceedingly stylish, generally embellished with an elaborate and beautifully carved wooden balcony, resplendent with geraniums.

As befits a countryside famed for its cattle, Cantabria's green and pleasant land has a prodigious rainfall – a climate sharply divided by the high peaks of the Sierra Cantabrica, from the start of the great inland plateau, which can often look desert-like by comparison. Mist often veils the tops of the hills around Bárcena, creating a soft colour scheme that harmonizes with the wood and stone, while the rushing sound of the Argoza provides a fitting accompaniment.

*T*he houses of Bárcena (these pages) *seem caught in timelessness, their peace broken only by the gentle burbling of the stream that runs beside the village. Many of the houses have ground-floor byres which are still used to house the cattle during the winter months.*

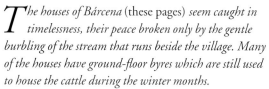

Betanzos A CORUÑA

GALICIA'S ROCKY COAST is pierced by a series of *rías*, fjord-like estuaries that run deep inland between low-lying hills. Betanzos has its own *ría*, fed by two rivers that curl around its ancient citadel to meet: the Mendo and the Mandeo. The Roman occupiers, who built Brigantium Flavium here on the site of an ancient Celtic village, established the first harbour. Trade boomed through the centuries, and at one time the port of Betanzos rivalled that of A Coruña. Unfortunately, the rivers that brought so much prosperity also brought large quantities of silt, and by the eighteenth century the *ría* had become impassable to cargo traffic.

Despite being left high and dry, the merchant families of Betanzos continued to flourish, marketing the grain produced in the fertile Mariñas valley, which lies inland. Their mansions line the narrow streets that run steeply down to the west, overlooking the former harbour. Many of these display that particularly Galician form of ostentation, the *solana*, or sun-gallery, which

tempers the Spanish love of the sun with due respect for the rough weather rolling in from the Atlantic.

Other fine buildings, private, public and ecclesiastical, overlook the activities on the main square, the huge and bustling Praza de los Hermanos García Naveira, whose huge expanse resounds most afternoons to the joyful voices of children, kicking footballs and careering about on tiny bicycles. Towards the top of the ancient citadel, shady streets lead to quieter and smaller squares, and a trio of fine Gothic churches: the sturdy and monastic basilica of San Francisco, the graceful Santa María del Azogue, and the fifteenth-century Santiago, slightly above. Santa María takes the latter part of its name from an ancient *souk* that once flourished in the adjoining square – a curiosity, as the Muslim invaders barely made it as far as Galicia, a part of Spain that remained largely untouched by the Moorish influence of the south.

Though now silted up, the harbour of Betanzos was once the centre of a thriving port, with houses ostentatiously embellished with glassed-in balconies (opposite and above). Its main benefactors, the two brothers Naveira, who returned to the town after making their fortunes in Argentina, are celebrated by a statue in the main square (above).

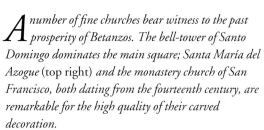

A number of fine churches bear witness to the past prosperity of Betanzos. The bell-tower of Santo Domingo dominates the main square; Santa María del Azogue (top right) *and the monastery church of San Francisco, both dating from the fourteenth century, are remarkable for the high quality of their carved decoration.*

Overleaf

Betanzos presents several different faces to the visitor: a narrow alley traces a dog-leg course along the side of the church of Santiago; a parade of merchants' houses, each topped by its glassed-in balcony or solana, *which look westwards to the site of the once busy port.*

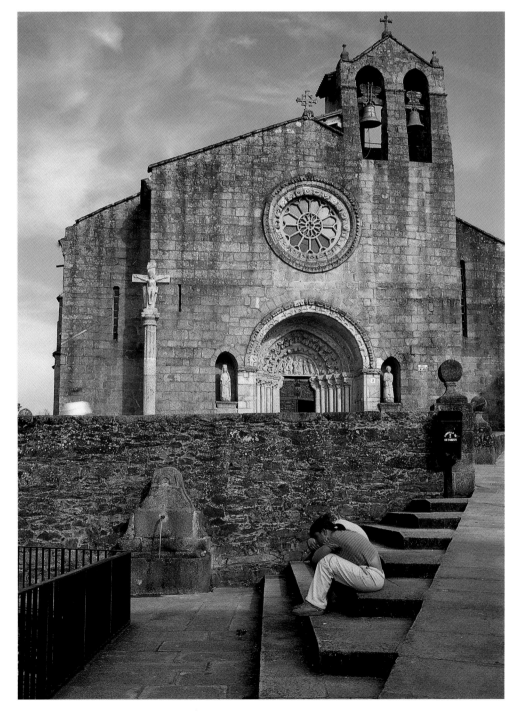

The curative powers of the waters of Lourdes are commemorated in this grotto in the church of Santiago (above). *Confrontation with Islam is remembered in the tympanum of the same church, which incorporates a carving of St. James on horseback as slayer of the Moors* (top). *Another reminder of the Moorish influence is the name of the church of Santa María del Azogue* (right), *which is derived from* souk, *'market-place' in Arabic. The niches on either side of the main portal contain statues of the Virgin Mary and of the Archangel Gabriel.*

Ituren NAVARRA

There is little indication in the September sunshine over the Ezburra valley of the rigours of the winter to come. But the expectation of the cold and snow is already there in the overhanging eaves, window shutters and thick walls (these pages).

IT WOULD BE MISLEADING to describe Navarra as suffering from a split personality; that would be an over-simplification of its madly complicated divisions. Despite these, however, the Navarrese seem to get along very well with each other, and not only during the yearly nine-day meltdown in Pamplona, when much of rural Navarra descends on the capital to go wild for the nine days of Los Sanfermines. Historically, the region has remained somewhat separate from the rest of Spain, often cultivating relations with France for political advantage. But the clearest division in Navarra is geographical: the great leap from the lushest of alpine valleys, in the north-west, close to the foothills of the Pyrenees, and the near-desert rockscapes of the south-east, south of Pamplona. Less than one hundred kilometres, for example, separates Olite (page 182) and Ituren; the latter, however, is firmly in the Pyrenean camp, and its culture as well as its language is shared with the Basque region of Guipúzcoa to the north.

Three hamlets make up the district of Ituren: the village itself, and neighbouring Aurtitz and Latsaga. All the houses of these valleys look ready to withstand huge falls of snow; gabled roofs with huge eaves overhang surprisingly delicate carved wooden balconies. In fact, extremes of weather are rare, with the coast not far away and even the steep surrounding hills not exceeding a modest 1,000 metres or so. In the centre of Ituren, the Plaza Mayor is overlooked by a stately sixteenth-century Casa Consistorial.

There is usually a lively game of pelota in progress, the Basque cousin of Eton fives, although the youth in these parts choose to play the hard ball bare-handed, unlike the young English gentlemen who protect their palms with a padded glove. Such hardiness of the local youth is

consistent with the sporting activities of their fathers and older brothers, whose ideas of friendly competitive sports include log-chopping and boulder-lifting. Evidence of a split in the Navarrese personality might be inferred from the willingness of these burly men to dress up in sheepskins, don conical hats adorned with ribbons, wave horsehair switches and march from village to village wiggling their backsides to ring the huge cowbells attached to them. Not surprisingly, the evil spirits that these *zanpantzars*, held each January, are intended to scare away, are rarely seen in the valleys.

There is an air of spaciousness about the village and its surroundings (these pages): *plenty of pasturage for the ponies and plenty of scope for the traditional pleasures of childhood – hanging out by the river or joining in a game of* pelota, *the Basque version of handball.*

Llanes ASTURIAS

*N*ow relying less on the diminishing activities of its fishing fleet, Llanes is reclaiming its position as a coastal resort. The antiquated lighthouse (opposite) now acts as a beacon mainly to pleasure craft, sailing into harbour past a novel artwork, Los cubos de memoria, *created by Basque artist Agustín Ibarrola* (above).

LLANES is well positioned to justify its claim to be the premier resort of the Asturias. It is right on the prettiest part of the coast, and a subsidiary branch of the coastal mountains, an attraction to a new breed of green tourist, lies a mere six kilometres inland. When seaside holidays became big business at the end of the nineteenth century, Llanes was ready; by 1905 it had the all-important railway link, followed shortly by a casino and a string of luxurious villas, embellished with every imaginable decorative motif. Some of these are derelict, the paintwork mercifully faded; many have been painstakingly restored to their original gaudiness.

The entire harbour, looking for a new lease of life after the decline of a previously busy fishing industry, has been recently rebuilt. Spacious *paseos* have been incorporated along the new sea walls, from which the villagers can look down on the pleasure craft moored in the harbour. This new construction contrasts very pleasantly with the older part of the village, still dominating the scene from a slight eminence and graced with a long row of nineteenth-century merchant houses with fine glazed balconies. Higher, behind the substantial Basilica de Santa María, lie the remains of the palace of the dukes of Estrada, an uninhabited yet stylish shell since the night in 1808 when the locals set fire to it, upset by rumours that the noble owners, or the nobility in general, were preparing to make a deal with Napoleon, whose armies were threatening to invade. An unexpected survival is the original lighthouse, reached along the spanking new Paseo San Anton, all smooth lines and smart street furniture. This delightfully low-tech device is still in operation; no fresnel lens or rotating halogen, but inside the plain glass dome a giant bulb literally flicks on and off. It can't be visible very far out to sea, but it certainly sends a strong signal to the houses across the street, whose bedroom windows are screened by adroitly planted trees.

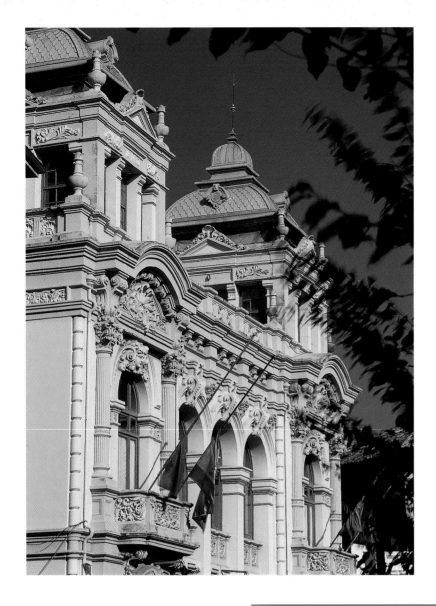

*B*ehind the thirteenth-century walls (right), *it is possible to gauge the extent of Llanes' appeal to the wealthy on holiday from the fin-de-siècle glories of the casino* (above) *and the fanciful detailing of some of the villas* (above right). *Even the well-stocked kiosk* (opposite) *seems to suggest that this is a place of some sophistication.*

Still and very architectural, with highly contrasting areas of light and shade, the Plaza Christo Rey has a theatrical air (these pages). Dominating it at the highest point of the village's medieval quarter is the basilica of Santa María del Concaya.

Olite NAVARRA

SOUTH OF PAMPLONA, the countryside of Navarra changes rapidly. By the time the visitor reaches Olite, the green and wooded foothills of the Pyrenees to the north seem like a distant memory, and the gently undulating, arid plain puts one firmly in Spain. The border with France may feel distant, but it is in fact only a matter of seventy kilometres away, and the powerful succession of kings that ruled over this fiercely independent region usually had strong links with the nobility of France.

Olite was traditionally a favoured residence of the kings of Navarra, and in the thirteenth century Thibault I set up his court here, building a royal palace at the edge of the old Roman settlement. This Castillo Viejo, which now houses the local Parador, was considered too limited for his descendant Carlos III ('El Noble'), who came to the throne at the beginning of the fifteenth century. His enlargement of the royal palace transformed the layout of the village. Carlos had been brought up in France as well as Spain, so he was well aware of the great houses his noble kinsmen and their monarchs were beginning to build in the Gothic style, especially in their new playground along the Loire. By the time Carlos' French architects and Moorish craftsmen had finished, the resulting confection formed a huge complex of state-rooms and living quarters, with a monumental sky-line punctuated by no fewer than fifteen towers. The spacious terraces of the upper floors, the great salons, and the hanging gardens above the village immediately recall the Chambord of François I; the defensive elements of castle design had finally ceded to more decorative impulses. Every taste was catered for in the new buildings, which eventually grew to accommodate a small community. As well as the gardens full of tender exotics and citrus trees, kept fruitful by an elaborate irrigation system, there was a menagerie, with a lions' den and an aviary, of which the remains can still be seen.

Besides such magnificence, the village must have looked dwarfed and much diminished. But Olite eventually prospered in its own right, becoming a major centre of wine production long after the departure of the last Navarrese kings.

For a place of modest size, Olite has a grandeur all its own, conferred upon it by the massive palace of Carlos III, who first ordered its building in 1406. The towers and battlements, where courtiers once strolled amid Gothic splendour, tower above the rooftops below and even dwarf the parish church of San Pedro (opposite *and* above).

*M*uch influenced by the design of the châteaux which his French kinsmen were building and embellishing along the Loire, Carlos ('El Noble') demanded additions like corbelled towers (above left) for the walls of his palace. Other decoration took the form of improbably delicate tracery in the stonework (left). The church of Santa María, adjoining the castle and previously secondary to that of San Pedro, received the most elaborate facelift in the form of Gothic ornament in the French style (above *and* opposite).

*B*elow the castle, there are plenty of dwellings which display *their own exuberance and sense of importance, like these merchant's houses* (opposite *and* above left). *The presence of the castle, though, is inescapable; its seemingly medieval gateway* (left), *however, scarcely indicates what delights lie within, like this little roof garden* (above).

Pasai Donibane (Pasajes) GUIPÚZCOA

VICTOR HUGO, that highly mobile proto-tourist, was greatly taken with Pasajes – so much so, that he spent most of the summer of 1842 here, writing of 'a canvas of high green hills, a line of piled-up houses,' and of 'an inescapable happiness'. Thus he enthused on his first sight of Pasajes, or Pasaia as it is known in the Basque language. The Bay of Pasaia could more properly be called a cove, by reason of its narrow entrance and mountainous surrounding hills. Snugly defended from the Bay of Biscay, then, it played a pre-eminent role in the seafaring history of the Basque people, while plentiful timber to hand encouraged the development of ship-building around the harbour. In a varied existence, Pasaia has been a port for merchant shipping in medieval times, a base for transatlantic whaling expeditions, a starting point for the Spanish Armada, and a home for the deep-sea cod fleets of recent times. All these functions have had to squeeze themselves into the narrow available space around the water's edge, and it is an arduous map-reading exercise for visitors to make their way round to the oldest and most traditional of the harbour communities, Pasai Donibane (Pasajes San Juan).

Here, the old layout of the place has remained unchanged, with very good reason. A single street, the Calle San Juan, is wedged between the towering hill of Jaizkibel and the water's edge. On the inner side of the street, the old houses lead a crepuscular existence under the shadow of the almost vertical hill; on the waterfront, their neighbours make the best use of their open outlook. Victor Hugo's old house, for example, is light and airy, with a wooden balcony on each of its three floors and, at water level, its own jetty. It looks over the bustling scene towards its neighbour on the opposite bank. Pasai San Pedro is a harbour community of equal antiquity, but which has had the room to expand, resulting in a quite sizeable, modern town. Not that the worldly sibling and the isolated Donibane have become estranged from one another: the tiny stand-up ferry, plying between the two in the manner of the Venetian *traghetto* over the Grand Canal (and covering about the same distance), does a brisk trade in foot passengers, especially around lunch-time, when San Pedro's business community can escape from the twentieth century, sit above the water on a shaded wooden terrace, and enjoy the excellent local seafood.

This village, strung out along a narrow shoreline beneath a steep wooded hill (opposite) *is best viewed from its more commercial neighbour of Pasai San Pedro, a short boat ride away. Some of the older houses* (above) *testify to its antiquity as a port and harbour.*

Ribadavia OURENSE

AWAY FROM THE COAST, a different Galicia presents itself. In the hill district of Ribeira, shady lanes weave between stone walls which enclose impossibly tiny parcels of land. Nevertheless, the enclosures are well worth the effort of cultivation; from them come the Ribeiro white wines, the first choice of Galicians to wash down the seafood that they consume with understandable gusto. And at the centre of this area, at the confluence of the Miño and the Avia, stands Ribadavia.

The walls built during the fourteenth and fifteenth centuries largely survive; three of the original five gates still guard the ways in and out. As well as forming a natural mercantile centre, Ribadavia was of political significance; for a brief period during the eleventh century it was the capital of Galicia. From around that time, the monasteries of the district, which owned large tracts of vineyard, helped to organize the production of wine and stimulate its export. Even now, the village is well endowed with churches. There are eight in all to discover, three of them tucked tightly inside the old walls. One of the oldest, beside the Porta Nova, was dedicated to those members of the sizeable Jewish community who converted to Christianity in order to avoid expulsion after the edict of the Reyes Católicos in 1492. As they had played a major part in the mercantile life of Ribadavia, and their community was one of the largest in northern Spain, a considerable number chose conversion over expulsion, and the church of the Magdalena was dedicated for their worship. Their former synagogue survives in front of the church, converted into a merchant's house. Less remains of the original castle of the counts of Ribadavia,

A stroll through Ribadavia's
warren of streets (above) *will
disclose plentiful glimpses of its many
churches and especially of their very
varied bell-towers: San Juan* (above
right); *the Baroque front of
Romanesque Santiago* (right); *and,
outside the walls, the convent church
of Santo Domingo* (opposite).

although its remains, built into the rock at the
highest point of the village, make a pleasant place
for a stroll, with views over the river. The castle
was allowed to fall into disrepair after the family
moved into a stylish seventeenth-century mansion
that still looks over the Plaza Mayor.

As well as enjoying renown for its wine
production, this area is also much visited for the
hot-water springs that rise from its chalky soil. An
agreeable break in the serious business of
enjoying Galicia's gastronomic delights is to bask
in the therapeutic waters of one of the diminutive
spas, all surrounded by ripening of the vines.

*O*ne water supply to the village, now used only by cattle, stands humbly to the side of the magnificent Colegiata (opposite), the jewel of the Cantabrian Romanesque style. Its main door is surmounted by a pediment with carvings of the Apostles and the martyr St. Juliana.

Santillana del Mar

CANTABRIA

SOME PLACES, like some people, are born lucky, and the little village of Santillana certainly gives the impression that prosperity is its natural state. It is easy to imagine how its position, in a shallow dip between low hills of woodland and rich pasture, must have attracted the eye of its first recorded settlers. These were a group of monks who established themselves there in the ninth century, dedicating a shrine for the preservation of the relics of St. Juliana. This community, benefiting from farm revenues as well as the patronage of nobility and royalty, grew to be the richest and most famous abbey in Cantabria. Its fortunes were further enhanced by its proximity to the pilgrimage route to Santiago de Compostela; many pilgrims made the detour to visit the saint's relics.

During this time, the present Colegiata was built, the largest church on the northern coast, still resplendent with its huge Romanesque south door, presided over by a figure of St. Juliana. The fifteenth century brought a decline in the abbey's fortunes and power passed to the local nobility; their efforts to wrest control from the abbot were formalized by the granting of the first marquisate of Santillana by King Juan II in 1445. The building of numerous stately houses by other noble families had the happy effect of raising the prestige of Santillana, without spoiling the intimate scale of the place. The village really consists of one street, dipping down towards the principal spring for watering the cattle, which stands before the massive south façade of the Colegiata. Along the street a dozen or so mansions of the nobility were built; as one contemporary observer accurately noted, they were 'great not in their size but in their pretensions'. This main street was joined later by another which led to a market square, forming a 'Y'. This square, the present Plaza Ramón Pelayo, boasts two semi-martial Gothic towers, as well as the finest of the mansions, the seat of the Barreda-Bracho family, now turned into the most atmospheric among the region's Parador hotels. Dwindling fortunes among the nobility were somewhat restored when the colonial adventures of younger scions brought wealth from the Americas to embellish afresh the stately mansions. And finally, just as the prestige of the noble families was on the decline during the nineteenth century, Santillana's extraordinary cultural significance was recognized by the state, and a concerted effort was made to preserve and renovate its buildings.

*M*any of Santillana's houses seem much too grand for a community so modest in size (these pages), *evidence of the extent to which it was once a centre of the local nobility. Seigneurial coats of arms abound on the façades, including that of the Archduchess of Austria.*

FURTHER READING

Brenan, Gerald, *The Face of Spain*, London, 1950.
– *South from Granada*, London, 1957.
– *The Spanish Labyrinth*, Cambridge, 1943.
Carr, Raymond, *The Spanish Tragedy – The Civil War in Perspective*, London, 1977.
Carr, Raymond (ed.), *Spain. A History*, Oxford, 2000.
Cervantes, Miguel de (trans. J.M. Cohen), *Don Quixote*, Harmondsworth, 1950.
Chetwode, Penelope, *Two Middle-aged Ladies in Andalusia*, London, 1963.
Elliott, J. H., *Imperial Spain 1469–1716*, London, 1963.
Facaros, Dana and Pauls, Michael, *Spain* (Cadogan Guide series), London, 1987.
Fletcher, Richard, *Moorish Spain*, London, 1992.
Jacobs, Michael, *Andalucia* (Pallas Guide series), London, 2000.
Lee, Laurie, *A Moment of War*, London, 1991.
– *A Rose for Winter – Travels in Andalucia*, London, 1955.
– *As I Walked Out One Midsummer Morning*, London, 1963.
Morris, Jan, *Spain*, London, 1979.
Orwell, George, *Homage to Catalonia*, London, 1938.
Thomas, Hugh, *The Spanish Civil War*, London, 1961.

Opposite
*H*owever grand the mansions and the Colegiata of Santillana may appear, in one quiet corner the washing hangs out to dry and no doubt there is some modest cultivation within the small private garden.

FOOD IN SPAIN

WHEN IT COMES TO THE PLEASURES OF THE TABLE, once again the story in Spain is one of extraordinary diversity. One factor that is common to all the country's regions, though, is that everyone, everywhere, loves to go out to eat. Most of Spain is blessed with that enviable precondition for spontaneous sociability: a friendly climate. The long warm evenings of the summer see almost every restaurant and café full to capacity, but at lunch-time too the Spaniards will be found enjoying a serious meal, as befits the co-inventors, with their Mediterranean neighbours, of that civilized institution, the *siesta*.

The local wines are very good value, at whatever level of distinction – and some of the specialized producers of La Rioja are creating world-class vintages. As well as costing less than on the other side of the Pyrenees, the consistency and quality control, many would say, makes it far more difficult to choose an unfamiliar wine and come up with something disagreeable. The Sherries from the western part of Andalucía don't have to compete with anything else; they are of course a classic that 'merits the detour', to drink a *copa*, or several, on its home territory.

Meats of all sorts, including wild game and fowl, are to be found all over Spain, although the heartiest stews belong far inland from the coasts, where the locals have learnt the hard way how to survive the winters with the help of their animals. *Jamón* is a national institution served all over Spain, and the veneration with which it is carved and presented will cease to puzzle after the first mouthful.

As for seafood, where to begin? Perhaps on the Mediterranean coast of Andalucía, where it is wonderful, past Catalunya where it is fabulous, and Cantabria where it is amazing, to Galicia where it is sublime. This is a view based on pure subjectivity! A huge number of Spanish holidaymakers do head northwest, though…. and the sight of barnacle-gatherers braving the Atlantic surf to pluck the choicest *percebes* from the streaming rocks… well, that's my kind of heroism.

Diversity is where this book started, and where it should end. Why content oneself with a single experience when a whole realm of different experiences is there for the asking? Yes, this is the very Spanish philosophy of the *tapas* bar, where one can simultaneously chat, drink, listen to music and nibble one's way round a wonderful gastronomic spectrum!

*S*kilful carving of a carefully aged
ham is a near-holy rite in Spain,
where the ubiquitous jamón *is
almost a national symbol, beloved
throughout the country. The choicest
variety is Jamón Ibérico, from the
highlands of Extremadura, served
here at El Rinconcillo* (above left).

*S*eville's finest and oldest *tapas
bar, El Rinconcillo, dates back to
1670* (above).

*V*alencia can claim the credit for
the invention of *paella, *which
uses the plentiful seafood of the
nearby Mediterranean and the rice
that is grown traditionally on the
Albufera lagoon, to the south of
the city* (left).

201

TRAVELLERS' GUIDE

While every effort has been made to ensure that the information given in the following entries is correct, the author and the publisher cannot be held responsible for any inadvertent inaccuracies.

TOURIST OFFICES

Spanish National Tourist Office
22–23 Manchester Square, London W1U 3PX, UK; tel. +44(0) 207 486 8077. (www.tourspain.co.uk)

Tourist Office of Spain
666 Fifth Avenue, 35th Floor, New York, NY 10103, USA; tel. +1(212) 265 8822. (www.okspain.org)

Tourist Office of Spain
2 Bloor Street West, Suite 3402, Toronto, Ontario, Canada M4W 3E2; tel. +1(416) 961 3131. (www.tourspain.toronto. on.ca)

EASTERN SPAIN

Albarracín TERUEL

WHERE TO STAY
Hotel-Restaurant *Casa de Santiago*, c. Subida a las Torres, 11; tel. (978) 700316.
Hotel-Restaurant *La Casona del Ajimez*, c. San Juan, 2; tel. (978) 710321.
Hostel *Santo Cristo*, cno. Santo Cristo, 17; tel. (978) 700301.
WHERE TO EAT
Restaurant *Mesón del Gallo*, c. Puentes, 1; tel. (978) 700281.
Restaurant *El Portal*, c. Portal de Molina; tel. (978) 700390.
Restaurant *Le Rincón del Chorro*, c. del Chorro, 15; tel. (978) 710112.
INFORMATION
C. Diputación, 4; tel. (978) 710251.

Alquézar HUESCA

WHERE TO STAY
Hotel *Santa María*, c. Arrabal; tel. (974) 318436.
Hotel *Villa del Alquézar*, c. Pedro Arnal Cavero, 12; tel. (974) 318416.
Hostel-Restaurant *Fonda Narbona*; tel. (974) 318078.
WHERE TO EAT
Restaurant *Casa Gervasio*; tel. (974) 318282.
Restaurant *Mesón del Vero*; tel.(974) 318074.
INFORMATION
Ctra. Barbastro; tel. (974) 318940.

Besalú GIRONA

WHERE TO STAY
Hotel-Restaurant *Els Jardins de la Martana*, c. Pont, 2; tel. (972) 590009.
Hotel-Restaurant *Siqués 'Cal Parent'*, avda. Lluis Companys, 6-8; tel. (972) 590110.
Hotel-Restaurant *Venencia*, c. Major, 6; tel. (972) 591257.

WHERE TO EAT
Restaurant *Els Fogons de Can Llaudes*, Prat de san Pere, 6; tel. (972) 590858.
Restaurant *Pont Vell*, c. Pont Vell, 24; tel. (972) 591027.
INFORMATION
Pl. Llibertat, 2; tel. (972) 591240.

Cadaqués GIRONA

WHERE TO STAY
Hotel-Restaurant *Llane Petit*, c. Dr Bartomeus, 37; tel. (972) 251020.
Hotel-Restaurant *Port Lligat*, pl. de Port Lligat; tel. (972) 258162.
WHERE TO EAT
Restaurant *El Barroco*, c. Nou; tel. (972) 258632.
Restaurant *Es Baluard*, riba Nemesio Llorens, 2; tel. (972) 258184.
Restaurant *La Galiota*, c. Narcís Monturiol, 9; tel. (972) 258187.
INFORMATION
C. Cotxe, 2; tel. (972) 258315.

Deià MALLORCA

WHERE TO STAY
Hotel-Restaurant *D'Es Puig*, c. Es Puig, 4; tel. (971) 639409.
Hotel-Restaurant *La Residencia*, Son Canals; tel. (971) 639011.
WHERE TO EAT
Restaurant *Sa Vinya*, c. Sa Vinya Vella, 3; tel. (971) 639500.
Restaurant *Sebastian*, c. Felip Bauzà, 2; tel. (971) 639417.
INFORMATION
Pl. de Sa Constituciò, 1, Soller (10 km northeast); tel. (971) 630200.

El Palmar VALENCIA

WHERE TO STAY
Hotel-Restaurant *Parador de el Saler* (3 km

A Coruña
Betanzos
GALICIA
Santiago de Compostela
Ourense
Ribadavia
Oviedo
Llanes
Santander
Santillana del Mar
ASTURIAS
CANTABRIA
Bárcena Mayor
Bilbao
EUZKADI
Pasai Donibane
Ituren
Pamplona
FRANCE
Leon
NAVARRA
ANDORRA
Cadaqués
Burgos
Ebro
Olite
Sos del Rey Católico
LA RIOJA
Huesca
Alquézar
Besalú
Rupit
Girona
CASTILLA Y LEÓN
CATALUÑYA
Valladolid
Soria
Calatañazor
Zaragoza
ARAGÓN
Montblanc
Barcelona
Salamanca
Pedraza
Segovia
Tarragona
Ávila
Candelario
La Huetre
Madrid
Albarracín
Teruel
Peñíscola
MENORCA
Tagus
Toledo
La Guardia
COMUNIDAD VALENCIANA
Cáceres
Guadalupe
EXTREMADURA
CASTILLA Y LA MANCHA
Valencia
El Palmar
Deià
Palma de Mallorca
MALLORCA
Ciudad Real
Almagro
IBIZA
Alicante
Almonaster la Real
MURCIA
Córdoba
Guadalquivir
Jaén
Alcalá la Real
Huelva
Moguer
Sevilla
ANDALUCÍA
Granada
Sanlúcar de Barrameda
Grazalema
Capileira
Cádiz
Medina Sidonia
Malaga
Vejer de la Frontera
Mediterranean
PORTUGAL

0   50   100 Miles
0   50   100   150 Km.

---

north), avda. de los Pinares, 151;
tel. (961) 611186.

Hotel-Restaurant *Patilla* (7 km north),
c. Pinares, 10, el Saler;
tel. (961) 830382.

WHERE TO EAT

Restaurant *Bon Aire*, c. Caudete, 41; tel. (961)
620313.

Restaurant *Racó de l'Olla* (1.5 km north), ctra.
de el Saler; tel. (961) 620172.

INFORMATION

C. Paz, 48, Valencia (20 km north);
tel. (963) 986422.

Montblanc TARRAGONA

WHERE TO STAY

Hotel-Restaurant *Ducal*, c. Francesc Macia, 11;
tel. (977) 862448.

Hotel-Restaurant *Fonda Cal Blasi*, c. Alenyà,
11; tel. (977) 861336.

WHERE TO EAT

Restaurant *El Call de Montblanc*, c. San Josep,
15; tel. (977) 863224.

Restaurant *Fonda Colom*, ctra. de Civadeira, 5;
tel. (977) 860153.

Restaurant *El Molí del Mallol*, c. Muralla
Santa Anna, 2; tel. (977) 860591.

INFORMATION

C. Miguel Alfonso; tel. (977) 861733.

Peñíscola CASTELLÓN

WHERE TO STAY

Hotel-Restaurant *Hosteria del Mar*, avda. Papa
Luna, 18; tel. (964) 480600.

Hostel-Restaurant *Hostal del Duc*, c.
Fulladosa, 10; tel. (964) 480768.

Restaurant *Altamíra*, c. Principe, 3;
   tel. (964) 480038.
Restaurant *Mirador*, c. Santos Martires, 15;
   tel. (964) 489834.
Restaurant *Simó*, c. Porteta, 5;
   tel. (964) 480620.
Restaurant *Vista al Mar*, c. Principe, 4; tel.
   (964) 481231.
INFORMATION
Paseo Maritimo; tel. (964) 480208.

Rupit BARCELONA

WHERE TO STAY
Hotel *Borell* (at Olot, 28 km north-east), c.
   Nónit Escubós, 8, Olot; tel. (972) 276161.
Hostel-Restaurant *Estrella*, pl. Bisbe Font, 1;
   tel. (938) 522005.
Hostel *El Repos*, c. Barbacana; tel. (938)
   522100.
WHERE TO EAT
Restaurant *Ca l'Estragués*, c. Eglésia, 4;
   tel. (938) 522006.
Restaurant *L'Hort d'en Roca*, pl. Era Nova;
   tel. (938) 522029.
INFORMATION
C. Lorenzana, 15, Olot (28 km north-east);
   tel. (972) 260141.

Sos del Rey Católico ZARAGOZA

WHERE TO STAY
Hotel-Restaurant *Parador de Sos del Rey
   Católico*, c. Arquitecto Sáinz de Vicuña, 1;
   tel. (948) 888011.
Hostel-Restaurant *Las Coronas*, c. Pons
   Sorolla, 1; tel. (948) 888408.
Hostel-Restaurant *Fonda Fernandina*, c.
   Emilio Alfaro; tel. (948) 888120.
INFORMATION
C. del Pino, 5; tel. (948) 888150.

*T*he restaurant El Barroco, in the
heart of the Cadaqués, was
a haunt of Salvador Dalí which he
redesigned in the 1970s. Its shady
courtyard is just the place to stop for
a refreshing glass of beer and some
local anchovies.

ANDALUCÍA

Alcalá la Real JAÉN

WHERE TO STAY
Hotel-Restaurant *Torrepalma*, c. Conde de
   Torrepalma, 2; tel. (953) 581800.
Pension *Río de Oro*, paseo de los Álamos, 4;
   tel. (953) 580337.
WHERE TO EAT
Restaurant *Casa Pedro*, avda. de Andalucía;
   tel. (953) 580483
Restaurant *Parada de Autobuses*, avda. de
   Andalucía; tel. (953) 582731.
INFORMATION
Paseo de los Álamos; tel. (953) 582217.

Almonaster la Real HUELVA

WHERE TO STAY
Hotel-Restaurant *Los Castaños* (at Aracena,
   22 km east), av. de Huelva, 5, Aracena;
   tel. (959) 126300.
Hostel *La Cruz*, c. José Antonio, 8; tel. (959)
   143135.
WHERE TO EAT
Restaurant *Casa García de Almonaster*, av.
   San Martin, 2; tel. (959) 143109.
Restaurant *Las Palmeras*, ctra. Almonaster;
   tel. (959) 143105.
INFORMATION
Pl. de San Pedro, Aracena; tel. (959) 128355.

Capileira GRANADA

WHERE TO STAY
Hotel Apartments *Finca los Llanos*, ctra.
   Sierra Nevada; tel. (958) 763071.
Pension *Mesón Poqueira*, c. Dr Castilla, 6;
   tel. (958) 763048.
Hostel-Restaurant *Paco López*, pl. J. Solis;
   tel. (958) 763076.
WHERE TO EAT :
Restaurant *Finca los Llanos*, ctra. Sierra
   Nevada; tel. (958) 763071.
Restaurant *Moraima*, c. Barranco de
   Poqueira; tel. (958) 763329.
INFORMATION
Pl. de la Libertad, Pampaneira (6 km south);
   tel. (958) 763127.

Grazalema CÁDIZ

WHERE TO STAY
Hotel-Restaurant *Parador de Ronda* (23 km
   east), pl. de España, Ronda;

A bodeguita *is the equivalent of a wine bar, but most serve* delicious *tapas* that can be eaten *en passant. Señor Romero's famous establishment is on Calle Antonia Díaz, just beside Seville's cathedral.*

tel. (952) 877500.
Hotel-Restaurant *Puerta de la Villa*, pl. Pequeña, 8; tel. (956) 132376.
Hotel-Restaurant *Villa Turistica*, ctra. Comarcal 344; tel. (956) 132136.
WHERE TO EAT
Restaurant *Cádiz el Chico*, pl. de España, 8; tel. (956) 132027.
Restaurant *El Pinsapar*, c. Dr Mateos Galgo, 22; tel. (956) 132202.
INFORMATION
Pl. de España, 11; tel. (956) 132225.

Medina Sidonia CÁDIZ

WHERE TO STAY
Hotel-Restaurant *Medina Park* (4 km east), ctra. Comarcal, 346; tel. (956) 410504.
Hotel-Restaurant *El Molino*, avda. Al-Andalus, 1; tel. (956) 410300.
Pension *Napoleón*, c. san Juan, 21; tel. (956) 410183.
WHERE TO EAT
Restaurant *Cádiz*, pl. España, 13; tel. (956) 410250.
Restaurant *El Castillo*, c. Ducado de Medina Sidonia; tel. (956) 410823.
Restaurant *Mesón Machín*, pl. Iglesia Mayor; tel. (956) 411347.
INFORMATION
Pl. Iglesia Mayor; tel. (956) 412404.

Moguer HUELVA

WHERE TO STAY
Hotel-Restaurant *Parador de Mazagón* (28 km south), ctra. Huelva-Matalascañas, Mazagón; tel. (959) 536300.
Pension *Platero*, c. Aceña, 4; tel. (959) 372159.
Hostel *Lis*, c. Andalucía; tel. (959) 370378.
Hostel *Pedro Alonso Niño*, c. Pedro Alonso Niño; tel. (959) 372392.
WHERE TO EAT
Restaurant *Cristóbal Molina*, c. Juan Ramón Jiménez, 1; tel. (959) 372473.
Restaurant *La Parrala*, plaza de las Monjas, 22; tel. (959) 370452.
Restaurant *Santa Clara*, c. Portocarrero; tel. (959) 370027.
INFORMATION
Pl. Cabildo, 1; tel. (959) 371898.

Sanlúcar de Barrameda CÁDIZ

WHERE TO STAY
Hotel-Restaurant *Guadalquivir*, Calzada del Ejército, 10; tel. (956) 360742.
Hotel-Restaurant *Los Helechos*, pl. Madre de Dios, 9; tel. (956) 361349.
Hotel-Restaurant *Tartaneros*, Tartaneros, 8; tel. (956) 385378.
WHERE TO EAT
Restaurant *Casa Bigote*, Bajo de Guía; tel. (956) 362696.
Restaurant *Mirador Doñana*, Bajo de Guía; tel. (956) 364205.
Restaurant *El Veranillo*, c. Barrios Masero; tel. (956) 362719.
INFORMATION
Calzada del Ejército; tel. (956) 366110.

Vejer de la Frontera CÁDIZ

WHERE TO STAY
Hotel-Restaurant *La Casa del Califa*, pl. de España, 16; tel. (956) 447730.
Hotel-Restaurant *Convento de San Francisco*, la Plazuela; tel. (956) 451001.
Hostel-Restaurant *La Posada*, avda. los Remedios, 21; tel. (956) 450258.
WHERE TO EAT
Restaurant *Mesón Judería*, arco de las Monjas; tel. (956) 447657.
Restaurant *Trafalgar*, pl. de España, 31; tel. (956) 447638.
Restaurant *La Vera Cruz*, c. Eduardo Shelly, 1; tel. (956) 193626.
INFORMATION
C. Marqués de Tamarón, 10; tel. (956) 450191.

THE HEART OF SPAIN

Almagro CIUDAD REAL

WHERE TO STAY
Hotel *Don Diego*, c. Bolaños, 1; tel. (926) 861287.
Hotel-Restaurant *Parador de Almagro*, Ronda de San Francisco, 31; tel. (926) 860100.
Pension *Angelines*, c. Franciscas, 7; tel. (926) 860278.
WHERE TO EAT
Restaurant *Calatrava*, c. Bolaños, 3; tel. (926) 861353.
Restaurant *El Corregidor*, pl. Fray Fernández de Córdoba, 2; tel. (926) 860648.

*T*here is nothing complicated about the best tapas – they simply use the very best ingredients. The tastiest sausages in Spain are said to come from the district of Salamanca – indeed, in times past, they bought fame and fortune to the hill village of Candelario.

Restaurant *La Cuerda*, pl. General Jorreto, 6; tel. (926) 882805.
INFORMATION
C. Bernarda, 2; tel. (926) 860717.

Calatañazor SORIA

WHERE TO STAY
Hotel-Restaurant *Mesón Leonor* (at Soria, 32 km east), paseo del Mirón, Soria; tel. (975) 220250.
Hostel-Restaurant *Calatañazor*, c. Real, 10-12; tel. (975) 183642.
Hostel-Restaurant *De la Villa*, c. Tirador, 11; tel. (975) 183284.
WHERE TO EAT
Restaurant *Palomar*, Travesia Tirador, 22; tel. (975) 183284.
INFORMATION
Pl. Ramon y Cajal, Soria; tel. (975) 212052.

Candelario SALAMANCA

WHERE TO STAY
Hotel-Restaurant *Cinco Castaños*, ctra. de la Sierra; tel. (923) 413204.
Hotel-Restaurant *Parador de Salamanca* (72 km north), Teso de la Feria, 2, Salamanca; tel. (923) 192082.
Hostel-Restaurant *El Cristi*, pl. de Béjar, 1; tel. (923) 413212.
WHERE TO EAT
Restaurant *Artesa*, c. Mayor, 57; tel. (923) 413111.
Restaurant *La Romana*, Núñez Losada, 4; tel. (923) 413272.
INFORMATION
C. Compania, 2, Salamanca; tel. (923) 268571.

Guadalupe CÁCERES

WHERE TO STAY
Hotel-Restaurant *Hospedería del Real Monasterio*, pl. Juan Carlos I; tel. (927) 367000.
Hotel-Restaurant *Isabel*, pl. Santa María de Guadalupe, 13; tel. (927) 367126.
Hostel-Restaurant *Cerezo II*, pl. Santa María de Guadalupe, 33; tel. (927) 154177.
WHERE TO EAT
Restaurant *Mesón el Cordero*, c. Alfonso Onceno, 27; tel. (927) 367131.
Restaurant *Taruta*, c. Convento, 16; tel. (927) 367301.

INFORMATION
Pl. Santa María de Guadalupe; tel. (927) 154128.

La Guardia TOLEDO

WHERE TO STAY
Hotel-Restaurant *El Cardenal* (at Toledo, 57 km west), paseo de Recaredo, 24, Toledo; tel. (925) 224900.
Hostel-Restaurant *La Purísima* (at Tembleque, 11 km south), ctra. N-IV; tel. (925) 145078.
Hostel-Restaurant *Torresmancha*, ctra. N-IV; tel. (925) 123090.
Motel *El Queso* (at Tembleque), ctra. N-IV; tel. (925) 145063.
WHERE TO EAT
Restaurant *Los Arcos* (at Dos Barrios, 12 km north), ctra. N-IV, at Dos Barrios; tel. (925) 122129.
Restaurant *Las Torres* (at Tembleque), c. Convento, 71, Tembleque; tel (925) 145148.
INFORMATION
Pta. de Bisagra, Toledo; tel. (925) 220843.

La Huetre CÁCERES

WHERE TO STAY
Hotel-Restaurant (at Vallejera de Riofrio, 68 km east), ctra. N-630, Vallejera de Riofrio; tel. (923) 404600.
Hostel-Restaurant *Los Angeles* (at Nunomoral, 9 km south-east), ctra. Coria-Salamanca,120, Nuñomoral; tel. (927) 434005.
Hostel-Restaurant *Montesol* (at Casares, 1 km south-east), c. Lindón, 7, Casares; tel. (927) 433025.
WHERE TO EAT
Restaurant *El Hurdano* (at Nuñomoral), la Fuente, Nuñomoral; tel. (927) 433012.
INFORMATION
Pl. de la Catedral, Plasencia; tel. (927) 423843.

Pedraza SEGOVIA

WHERE TO STAY
Hotel-Restaurant *De la Villa*, c. Calzada, 5; tel. (921) 508651.
Hotel *Posada de Don Mariano*, c. Mayor, 14; tel. (921) 509886.
Hostel-Restaurant *Hostería Pintor Zuloaga*, c. Matadero, 1; (921) 509835.

WHERE TO EAT
Restaurant *La Olma*, pl. del Ganado I; tel.
(921) 509981.
Restaurant *El Yantar de Pedraza*, pl. Mayor;
tel. (921) 509842.
INFORMATION
C. Real; tel. (921) 508666.

NORTHERN SPAIN

Bárcena Major CANTABRIA

WHERE TO STAY
Hotel-Restaurant (at Reinosa, 46 km south-
east), ctra. Tres Mares, Reinosa; tel. (942)
779250.
Hotel-Restaurant *Viar* (at Cabezón de la Sal,
32 km north), ctra. N-634, Cabezón de la
Sal; tel. (942) 702219.
Hostel-Restaurant *Venta la Franca*, c. la
Franca; tel. (942) 706067.
WHERE TO EAT
Restaurant *La Fontana*; tel. (942) 741211.
Restaurant *El Puente*; tel. (942) 741200.
INFORMATION
C. Botín, 1, Cabezón de la Sal; tel. (942)
700332.

Betanzos A CORUÑA

WHERE TO STAY
Hotel-Restaurant *Los Ángeles*, c. los Ángeles,
11; tel. (981) 771511.
Hostel-Restaurant *Barreiro*, c. Rollo, 6;
tel. (981) 772259.
WHERE TO EAT
Restaurant *Mesón O Pasatempo*, c. As
Mariñas, 23; tel. (981) 775022.
Restaurant *La Penela*, Rúa dos Ferradores, 21;
tel. (981) 773127.
Restaurant *San Andrés*, c. los Ángeles, 4;
tel. (981) 772044.
INFORMATION
Pl. de la Constitución, 1; tel. (981) 770100.

Ituren NAVARRA

WHERE TO STAY
Hostel-Restaurant *Aurtizko Ostatua*, c. Baja,
17; tel. (948) 450477.
Hostel *Plazaenea*, pl. de la Villa, 8; tel. (948)
450018.
WHERE TO EAT
Restaurant *Donamaria'ko Benta* (5 km south-

east), barrio de la Venta, 4, Donamaria; tel.
(948) 450708.
Restaurant *Olari* (at Irurita, 16 km east),
c. Pedro María Hualde;
tel. (948) 452254.
INFORMATION
Parque Natural del Señorio de Bertiz (at
Oieregi, 11 km east); tel. (948) 592421.

Llanes ASTURIAS

WHERE TO STAY
Hotel-Restaurant *Miraolas*, paseo de San
Antón; tel. (985) 400828.
Hotel-Restaurant *Sablon's*, Playa del Salón, 1;
tel. (985) 401987.
Pension *Los Pinos*, avda. los Gaviotas, 18;
tel. (985) 401117.
WHERE TO EAT
Restaurant *Covadonga*, c. Mañuel Cue, 6;
tel. (985) 400891.
Restaurant *Mirador de Toró*, Playa del Toró
(1km east); tel. (985) 400882.
INFORMATION
La Torre, c. Alfonso IX; tel. (985) 400164.

Olite NAVARRA

WHERE TO STAY
Hotel-Restaurant *Casa Zanito*, Rúa Mayor,
16; tel. (948) 740002.
Hotel-Restaurant *Merindad de Olite*, Rúa de
la Judería, 11; tel. (948) 740735.
Hotel-Restaurant *Parador de Olite*, pl. de los
Teobaldos, 2; tel. (948) 740000.
WHERE TO EAT
Restaurant *Gambarte*, Rúa de Seco, 15;
tel. (948) 740139.
Sidrería Erri Berri, Rúa del Fondo, 1;
tel. (948) 741116.
INFORMATION
C. Mayor, 1; tel. (948) 741703.

Pasai Donibane GUIPÚZCOA

WHERE TO STAY
Hotel-Restaurant *Gudamendi* (at San
Sebastián, 11 km west), paseo Gudamendi,
San Sebastián; tel. (943) 214000.
Hostel-Restaurant *Bahía*, c. Eskalantegi, 21;
tel. (943) 514450.
WHERE TO EAT
Restaurant *Casa Cámara*, c. San Juan, 79;
tel. (943) 523699.

A Galician delicacy: pimientas
de Padrón – *small green
peppers, roasted and served with
plenty of sea salt.*

As the sun goes down, dinner is prepared – an event which will occupy most of the Spanish evening.

Restaurant *Nicolasa*, c. San Juan, 59;
  tel. (943) 515469.
Restaurant *Txulotxo*, c. San Juan, 71;
  tel. (943) 523958.
Restaurant *Badiola*, c. San Juan, 18;
  tel. (943) 518415.
INFORMATION
C. San Juan, 63; tel. (943) 341556.

Ribadavia OURENSE

WHERE TO STAY
Hostel-Restaurant *Evencio*, avda. Rodriguez
  Valcárcel, 30;
  tel. (988) 471045.
Hostel-Restaurant *Oasis*, ctra. N-120;
  tel. (988) 471613.
Hostel-Restaurant *Plaza*, Praza Maior;
  tel. (988) 470576.
WHERE TO EAT
Restaurant *Caracas*, c. Calvo Sotelo, 6;
  tel. (988) 470110.

Restaurant *O Pucheiro*, c. Alvaro Cunqueiro, 3;
  tel. (988) 470621.
INFORMATION
Pl. Mayor, 7; tel. (988) 471275.

Santillana del Mar CANTABRIA

WHERE TO STAY
Hotel-Restaurant *Meson de Borleña* (25 km
  south-east), ctra. N-623;
  tel. (942) 597622.
Hotel-Restaurant *Parador de Gil Blas*, pl.
  Mayor; tel. (942) 818000.
Pension *Castio*, c. Castio;
  tel. (942) 818255.
WHERE TO EAT
Restaurant *Altamira*, c. Canton, 1;
  tel. (942) 818025.
Restaurant *Los Blasones*, pl. de la Gándara;
  tel. (942) 818070.
INFORMATION
C. Jesús Otero, 20; tel. (942) 818251.